W9-AVW-218

DATE DUE

551.57
ALL
 Allaby, Michael.
  Droughts

DATE DUE	BORROWER'S NAME	

551.57
ALL
 Allaby, Michael.
  Droughts

Morgan Twp. H.S. Library
 Valparaiso, IN 46383

36825000047868

DROUGHTS

DANGEROUS WEATHER

DROUGHTS

Michael Allaby

Facts On File, Inc.

DROUGHTS

Copyright © 1998 by Michael Allaby

All rights reserved. No part of this book may be reproduced or utilized in any form or by any means, electronic or mechanical, including photocopying, recording, or by any information storage or retrieval systems, without permission in writing from the publisher. For information contact:

Facts On File, Inc.
11 Penn Plaza
New York NY 10001

Library of Congress Cataloging-in-Publication Data

Allaby, Michael.
   Droughts / Michael Allaby.
      p.   cm. — (Dangerous weather)
   Includes index.
   ISBN 0-8160-3519-9 (alk. paper)
   1. Droughts. I. Title. II. Series: Allaby, Michael. Dangerous
weather.
QC929.24.A45   1997
551.57'73—dc21   97-9544

Facts On File books are available at special discounts when purchased in bulk quantities for businesses, associations, institutions or sales promotions. Please call our Special Sales Department in New York at 212/967-8800 or 800/322-8755.

You can find Facts On File on the World Wide Web at http://www.factsonfile.com

Text design by Richard Garratt
Cover design by Matt Galemmo
Illustrations by Richard Garratt

Printed in the United States of America

RRD FOF 10 9 8 7 6 5 4 3

This book is printed on acid-free paper.

Contents

What is a drought?   1

WHEN THE RAINS FAIL   3

Air movements in the tropics and subtropics   3

George Hadley and Hadley cells   8

Subtropical deserts   10

Adiabatic warming and cooling   12

Desert life   14

Polar deserts   20

Precipitation, evaporation, sublimation, and ablation   24

Evaporation, condensation, and the formation of clouds   28

Ocean currents and sea-surface temperature   31

The Coriolis effect   32

El Niño and La Niña   36

Jet streams and storm tracks   43

Blocking highs   47

Vorticity and angular momentum   48

WATER AND LIFE   51

Why plants need water   51

Water below ground   55

Wells and springs   59

How droughts are classified   64

Droughts of the past   66

Drought and soil erosion   72

   Soil erodibility   76

The Dust Bowl   76

The Sahel   82

Monsoons   87

   Global circulation of the atmosphere   91

COPING WITH DROUGHT   94

Dry-weather farming   94

Irrigation   99

Water for people   104

Water recycling and purification   108

Desalination   112

Water storage   116

Saving water   120

Will climate change bring more droughts or fewer?   121

   The solar spectrum   122

Index   127

DROUGHTS

What is a drought?

By May, the land across a belt in Africa along the southern edge of the Sahara Desert is parched. Those plants that survive are brown and withered after the long, dry winter months. Then, in June, the rains return. They are monsoon rains (see page 87), heavy and prolonged. Soon rivers flow through what had been dried beds. Everywhere seeds hidden in the soil during the dry season germinate. Shrubs and trees produce leaves. The landscape turns green. Nomadic peoples drive their herds and flocks toward the burgeoning pasture and farmers sow their crops. Here, the farming year must end in late October when the monsoon rains cease and the dry season returns. This belt stretches across all or part of Senegal, Mauritania, Mali, Burkina Faso, Niger, Chad, Sudan, and Ethiopia. It is called the Sahel.

For a few years in the 1960s, the monsoon rains were heavier than usual and prospects for the Sahel farmers seemed promising.

Figure 1: *Dried riverbed, Missouri, 1959.* (Print and Pictures Department, The Free Library of Philadelphia)

Then, in 1968 and 1969, the rains were light, and between 1970 and 1972 there was no rain at all. In 1973 the rain was sparse. There was no rain in 1974 and another light monsoon in 1975. Since then, the monsoons have been erratic, good in some years and poor in others.

This was the Sahel drought, a period of five years, from 1968 to 1973, during which rainfall was very low or, during the worst years of 1972 and most of 1973, nonexistent. By the time the drought was over perhaps as many as 200,000 people and four million cattle had died. That is what drought means.

It is not only the subtropics that are afflicted by drought. While the eastern United States endured blizzards early in 1996, in Kansas, Oklahoma, and Texas, farmers were being forced to sell cattle for a fraction of their usual value because they could not feed them. The winter wheat crop failed for lack of rain and there was very little grass. Between October 1995 and May 1996, 3.7 inches of rain fell in San Antonio, Texas, where the average rainfall for those eight months is 15.8 inches. The drought was so severe it brought fears of a return to the conditions of the Dust Bowl years (see page 76).

In 1995 Britain enjoyed a magnificent summer. The spring had been cool and wet, but at the end of June the weather changed. Temperatures rose, the Sun shone every day, and on one memorable day the Isle of Skye, off the west coast of Scotland, was the warmest place in Europe.

Clear skies meant there was no rain, however, and little by little the water level in reservoirs fell. Britain is densely populated and demand for water is high, especially in summer. Restrictions were imposed on the use of water over most of the country. It was made illegal to use lawn hoses and garden sprinklers. In some areas there were fears that water would actually be rationed, by cutting off domestic supplies at certain times of the day. Rationing was not introduced, but restrictions on water use remained in force through-out the fall and most of the winter. This, too, was a drought and as rainfall remained low through the winter and reservoir levels rose only slowly, there were warnings of a further drought in the summer of 1996.

Drought is not a word with a precise definition. Three weeks without rain can be enough to trigger a drought emergency in Britain. In other countries no one talks of a drought until several rainless months have passed. A drought is simply a period during which rainfall is unusually lower than the average for that time of year in that place, making water in such short supply that domestic and industrial users, farmers, and wildlife are affected.

The most obvious effect arises from the lack of water itself. Plants wilt, animals die from thirst, and crops fail. There is a secondary effect, however, that brings more immediate dangers. When vegetation has withered and dried out, the merest spark may be enough to set it ablaze as a forest, bush, or grass fire that can spread rapidly.

Early in 1996 dry conditions led to forest fires in New Mexico, Arizona, and Colorado, and there was even fire in Alaska, fueled by moss on the forest floor and fanned by winds gusting to 25 MPH. By June 6, the fire covered 37,000 acres, with flames up to 200 feet high in the spruce and birch forest. At least 150 buildings had been destroyed, 700 people had been forced to evacuate their homes, the 74 inmates at Point MacKenzie prison farm had been evacuated, and the only highway between Anchorage and Fairbanks was closed. There was so much smoke in Anchorage that officials issued an air quality alert.

People adjust to the climate where they live and generally experience difficulties only when the weather departs from its usual pattern. Ordinary weather may be good or bad, but it is tolerable for those used to it. It is extreme weather that brings hardship and danger. Drought is one kind of extreme weather and it can and does happen anywhere.

WHEN THE RAINS FAIL

Air movements in the tropics and subtropics

Oceans cover more than two-thirds of the surface of the Earth. Ours is a watery planet. Water evaporates from the oceans, condenses to form clouds, and falls as rain or snow. Some of that rain and snow falls over land, from where it returns to the sea, thus completing the cycle.

It does not fall on all land equally, however. Some regions receive very much more than others. Kisangani, in the Democratic Republic of Congo, receives on average 67 inches of rain a year, for example, and Timbuktu, in Mali, receives an average of only nine inches. Both cities are in Africa and far from the sea, Kisangani less than one degree north of the equator, Timbuktu just south of 17° N. The difference in latitude is about the same as that between St. Louis, Missouri, and Edmonton, Alberta, two North American inland cities. With an average annual rainfall of 39.4 inches, St. Louis has a climate more than twice as wet as that of Edmonton, with 17.3 inches, but Kisangani is more than seven times wetter than Timbuktu.

What makes the difference is not the latitudinal distance between the cities, but where that distance is located. The Democratic Republic of Congo lies close to the equator and Mali in the subtropics. Both North American cities lie in temperate latitudes.

All the energy the Earth receives comes from the Sun. Most of that radiation passes through the atmosphere and warms the surface of land and sea. Air is warmed by contact with the warm surface. In other words, the land and sea are heated from above, but the air is heated from below.

It is this solar energy that drives our climates, but sunshine does not fall everywhere with the same intensity. As the Earth orbits the Sun, you can picture the path it follows as marking out the edge of a flat disk (called the *plane of the ecliptic*). Earth is almost upright in relation to the disk and, as figure 2 shows, if you picture the equator as marking the circumference of a disk at right angles to the axis of rotation, and with its center at the center of the Earth, the plane of that disk is approximately aligned with the plane of the ecliptic. This means that at noon the Sun is directly overhead close to the equator and the sunlight falls more intensely in equatorial regions than in higher latitudes. Experiment 13 in volume 6 explains how you can demonstrate this for yourself.

Equatorial regions are therefore heated more strongly than other regions. Glance at a map of the world and you will see that for most of its length the equator crosses the oceans. Water is very abundant there, and because the surface is warmed strongly by the Sun, the rate of evaporation is high.

Figure 2: *Why the sun is overhead in the tropics.*

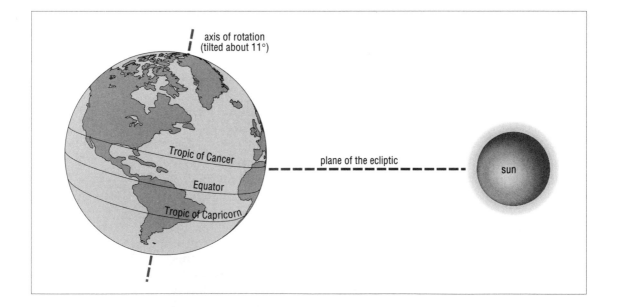

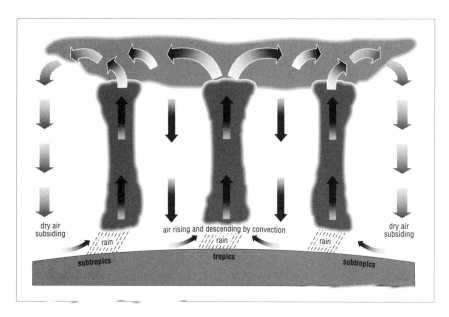

Figure 3: *Circulation of air over the tropics and subtropics.*

Air expands when it is warmed because its molecules absorb energy and move further apart. This reduces the density of the air. It is being warmed from below, so the air closest to the surface becomes less dense than the air immediately above it. This makes it rise and it continues to rise until it reaches a level where it is at the same density as the air around it. As it rises, the air cools *adiabatically* (see box on page 12).

Water evaporates into the warmed air and rises with it as water vapor. How much water vapor air can hold depends on the air temperature; warm air can hold more than cool air. The amount of vapor air holds as a proportion of the maximum it could hold at that temperature is called its relative humidity (RH), always ex-pressed as a percentage. Without any water vapor entering or leaving the air, as the temperature falls RH rises and as the temperature rises RH falls. If, for example, the RH of a certain mass of air at 70° F, is 50%, that same air will be saturated, with an RH of 100%, if it is cooled to 50° F. If it is warmed to 80° F, on the other hand, its RH will fall to 35%. The temperature at which air becomes saturated (its RH reaches 100%) is known as its *dew-point* tempera-ture. When this temperature is reached, water vapor will start to condense, and condensation is one way to measure dew-point temperature, described in experiment 11 in *A Chronology of Weather*.

Over the equator a lot of warm, moist air rises, and as it rises it cools. Soon it reaches its dew-point temperature. Water starts to condense, clouds form, and when the cloud droplets grow too large and heavy for the rising air currents to support them, they fall as rain. That is why rainfall is high in equatorial regions. Air rises in some places and between them sinking air brings dry weather, as shown in figure 3. Even over the equator it does not rain all the time.

Most of the rising air travels upward until it reaches the tropopause. This is a boundary, at a height of about 10 miles over the equator, above which the temperature and density of air do not decrease with height, so rising air is trapped beneath it. As figure 3 shows, once the air can rise no further it spills away from the equator, to the north and south. At this height the air temperature is usually between −94° F and −120° F, so it can hold almost no water vapor at all. It is extremely dry.

Fed constantly by an endless supply of rising air and chilled to a very low temperature, the high-level air becomes denser. As it moves away from the equator it meets air less dense than itself and sinks beneath it, all the way to the surface. Sinking air is compressed because the lower it descends the greater is the weight of all the air in the atmosphere above it. As it sinks and is compressed it warms adiabatically. By the time it reaches the surface the air is hot, but still extremely dry. Where it reaches the surface it creates dry, desert conditions.

Look again at a map of the world and you will see a belt of deserts in both hemispheres with their centers just outside the Tropics of Cancer (northern hemisphere) and Capricorn (southern hemisphere). These are the deserts produced by warm, dry, sinking air. The Sahara, Arabian Desert, Thar Desert of India, Australian Desert, Atacama Desert, and the desert of Central America are generated by this movement of air. However, it is not only in the tropics and subtropics that subsiding air produces deserts, and not all deserts are hot. Polar regions are also deserts, despite their deep covering of snow and ice (see page 20).

The desert belt is wider than it would be if the Earth were upright in relation to the plane of the ecliptic. In fact, its axis of rotation is tilted by about 11°. This tilt produces our seasons and also the tropics. There are two belts, one on either side of the equator, bounded by the highest latitude at which the noonday Sun is directly overhead on at least one day in the year. The Tropic of Cancer is at latitude 23°30' N and the Tropic of Capricorn at 23°30' S.

As the Earth orbits the Sun, its axial tilt remains constant and first one hemisphere is tilted towards the Sun, then the other. Figure 4 illustrates this, but with the tilt exaggerated to emphasize the effect it produces. In December, the southern hemisphere is tilted towards the Sun. At noon on December 21 the Sun is directly above the Tropic of Capricorn, and the southern hemisphere has its longest day. This is the southern midsummer day. On June 21, it is the northern hemisphere that is tilted towards the Sun, and at noon the Sun is directly above the Tropic of Cancer. This is the northern midsummer day. On March 21 and September 21, the Sun is directly overhead at the equator and both hemispheres receive an equal

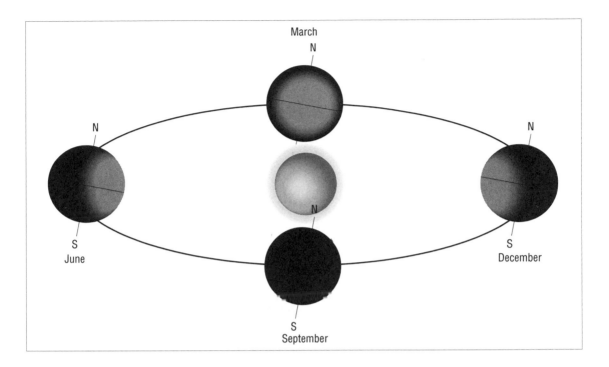

March
N

N

N

N

S
June

S
December

S
September

amount of sunlight, with equal hours of daylight and darkness in both. These are the spring and fall equinoxes.

Geographically, the equator is the line drawn on maps around the center of the Earth, equidistant from the two poles, but the climatic equator has to be defined rather differently, as the line joining all points where the noonday Sun is directly overhead. Because of the Earth's axial tilt, this line moves north in summer, south in winter, and coincides with the geographic equator only twice a year, at the equinoxes. The vertical movement of air by convection, illustrated in figure 3, is centered on the climatic equator rather than the geographic one, and it also moves north and south with the seasons. Since the region in which air is rising moves, so does the region in which subsiding air produces hot, dry conditions. This spreads the desert belts into higher latitudes than they would otherwise occupy.

Not all the deserts in the world result from this circulation of tropical and subtropical air. Deserts also occur in the deep interior of Asia, where the air reaching them has traveled so far over land as to have lost its moisture, and in the lee of mountains on the western sides of continents in midlatitudes. Since midlatitude weather systems move from west to east, these areas are dry because the air loses its moisture as it rises over the mountains. They are in the rain shadow of the mountains. The deserts to the east of the Rockies in the United States are of this type.

Figure 4: *Seasons and the Earth's orbit.*

George Hadley and Hadley cells

When European ships began venturing far from their home ports, into the tropics and across the equator, sailors learned that the trade winds are very dependable in both

Three-cell model of atmospheric circulation.

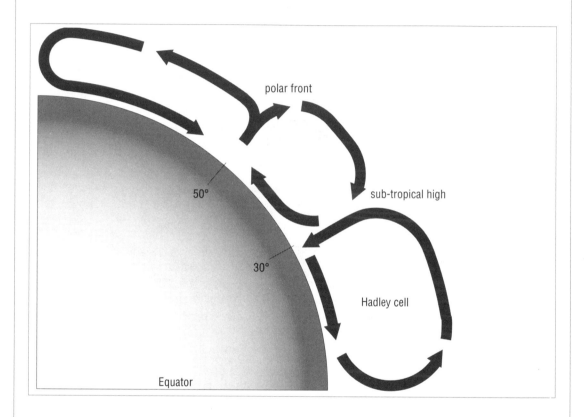

polar front

sub-tropical high

50°

30°

Hadley cell

Equator

You can demonstrate for yourself how easy it is to make air circulate convectively, rising in one place because it is warm and sinking in another because it is cool. Experiment 12 in volume 6 explains how to do it.

This is part of the mechanism by which warmth moves from the equator into higher latitudes, and it was discovered more than 250 years ago. At that time, no one was thinking of explaining why deserts are where they are, of course. That would have been much too ambitious a project, and in any case, another consequence of this circulation was of far greater importance. If air is rising, air must also be flowing in at low level to take its place. Air moving horizontally is a wind, and to either side of the equator the winds strength and direction. They made use of them, and by the end of the 16th century their existence was well known.

Many years passed, however, before anyone knew why the trade winds blow so reliably. Like many scientific explanations, this one developed in stages.

Edmund Halley (1656–1742), the English astronomer, was the first person to offer an explanation. In 1686 he suggested that air at the equator is heated more strongly than air anywhere else. The warm equatorial air rises, cold air flows in near the surface from either side to replace it, and this inflowing air forms the trade winds. If this were so, however, the trades either side of the equator would flow from due north and south. In fact, they flow from the northeast and southeast.

There the matter rested until 1735. In that year George Hadley (1685–1768), an English meteorologist, proposed a modification of the Halley theory. Hadley agreed that warm equatorial air rises and is replaced at the surface, but said that the rotation of the Earth from west to east swings the moving air, making the winds blow from the northeast and southeast.

Hadley was right about what happened, but not about the reason for it. This was discovered in 1856 by the American meteorologist William Ferrel (1817–91), who said the swing is due to the tendency of moving air to rotate about its own axis, like coffee stirred in a cup.

In accounting for the trade winds, Hadley had proposed a general explanation for the way heat is transported away from the equator. He suggested that the warm equatorial air moves at a great height all the way to the poles, where it descends. When this kind of vertical movement driven by heating from below occurs in a fluid, it is called a *convection cell*; the cell Hadley described is known as a *Hadley cell*.

The rotation of the Earth prevents a single, huge Hadley cell from forming. What really happens is more complicated. In various equatorial regions, warm air rises to a height of about 10 miles, moves away from the equator, cools, and descends between latitudes 25° and 30° N and S. These are the Hadley cells. When it reaches the surface in the tropics, some of the air flows back toward the equator and some flows away from the equator.

Over the poles, cold air descends and flows away from the poles at a low level. At about latitude 50° it meets air flowing away from the equatorial Hadley cells. Where the two types of air meet is called the *polar front*. Air rises again at the polar front. Some flows toward the pole, completing a high-latitude cell, and some flows toward the equator until it meets the descending air of the Hadley cell, which it joins.

There are three sets of cells in each hemisphere. This is called the *three-cell model* of atmospheric circulation by which warm air moves away from the equator and cool air moves toward the equator.

are very predictable. They blow from the northeast in the northern hemisphere and southeast in the southern and are so predictable that sailors called them the *trade winds*, because they were of great use to trading ships. It was the reliability of the trade winds that needed explaining, and the large-scale circulation of tropical air was the mechanism that supplied the explanation. Several scientists attempted the task, but the name most closely associated with this circulation is that of George Hadley (see box 8) and the tropical convection he described is called a *Hadley cell*.

It also explained something else of interest to sailors, which they called the *doldrums*. These are areas close to the equator where winds are almost always very light and variable in direction, and often no wind blows at all. Ships could be becalmed in them. They occur because converging trade-wind air also rises, quite gently, as it crosses the warm sea. Close to the climatic equator the air can be almost still because the air is moving vertically rather than horizontally. The result is the doldrums, on the eastern sides of the Atlantic and Pacific Oceans from October to June, but spreading far to the west from July to September. The doldrums also cover much of the equatorial Indian Ocean and western Pacific between October and December and in March and April.

Subtropical deserts

Deserts are dry. This is not to say it never rains. Sometimes it does, and heavily. When that happens, torrential rivers flow through what had been dried beds. Often there are widespread floods. Then the water soaks into the ground or evaporates and the land is parched once more. Clouds may appear in the sky, but they drift across it and disappear without producing rain. On average, clouds cover 10% of the sky over the Sahara in winter and 4% in summer.

In the harshest of deserts, long periods can pass when no rain falls. Iquique, in Chile, once went for 14 years without rain, but it has also received four inches of rain in a single day. At Wadi Halfa, in the Sahara, no rain fell for 19 years. When it does rain, such cities are often flooded because they lack storm drains to carry away surplus water.

These are exceptionally arid places, however, and provided there is some rain, low annual rainfall by itself is not enough to produce desert conditions. What matters is the *effective precipitation*. Rain must not only fall, but the land must trap and hold the water it receives. Whether or not it can do so depends on the rate at which water evaporates, so the effective precipitation is the amount of rainfall minus the amount of evaporation. If the annual amount of rainfall is less than the amount that could evaporate from the surface during the year, the ground will be short of water most of the time and a desert will develop.

Obviously, if the ground is very dry there will be little evaporation, because there is no water to evaporate. To resolve this difficulty, the rate of evaporation is calculated as the amount that would evaporate if the ground were saturated. This is quite easy to measure, and experiment 24 in *A Chronology of Weather* tells you how to do so and how to relate the evaporation rate to the air temperature.

Temperature is clearly important because water evaporates faster into warm air than into cold air. Deserts are less likely to form in cool than in hot climates, but regardless of temperature, anywhere with an average annual rainfall of less than 10 inches is likely to be desert because more than that amount of moisture can evaporate even into extremely cold air.

Divide the amount of rainfall in a particular area by the average temperature and the resulting figure indicates whether or not that area is a desert. You also need to know the time of year when most of the rain falls. Temperatures are higher in summer than in winter, so evaporation is higher in summer and more rain is needed to prevent a desert from forming. Rainfall distribution is allowed for by adjusting the formula. If most rain falls in winter, the formula is $r \div t$; if it falls mainly in summer, use $r \div (t + 14)$; and if the rainfall is distributed evenly throughout the year use $r \div (t + 7)$, where r is the rainfall in centimeters (to convert inches to centimeters multiply by 0.394) and t is the average temperature in degrees Celsius (°C = (°F − 32) × 5 ÷ 9). If the answer is less than 1, the area is desert. At In Salah, Algeria, for example, the average annual rainfall is 1.7 cm, falling mainly in winter, and the average temperature is 25.4° C. Applying the formula, $r \div t = 1.7 \div 25.4 = 0.07$. In Salah lies in a desert, in this case the Sahara. Phoenix, Arizona, has 19 cm of rain a year, distributed fairly evenly through the year, and the average temperature is 21.25° C. Applying $r \div (t + 7)$ gives $19 \div (21.25 + 7) = 0.7$. Phoenix lies in a desert, but its desert climate is less extreme than that of In Salah. You could use weather data for your own area (ask for them at the public library) to find out whether you live in a desert (you could also look out the window, but this way is more fun).

Tropical and subtropical deserts are so dry because the air over them is subsiding on the descending side of the tropical Hadley cell (see page 8). They are also hot, partly because they lie in low latitudes, but also because the air itself is hot. As it descends, it warms adiabatically (see box on page 12).

At least daytime temperatures are high. It is much cooler at night, especially in winter. In July, the hottest month, the average daytime temperature at In Salah is 113° F (and 122° F has been recorded), but at night it cools to 83° F. January is the coolest month, with an average daytime temperature of 69° F and a nighttime temperature of 43° F (and it can fall below freezing). This is a big difference, of 26–30° F, that varies little between summer and winter. In Philadelphia, in contrast, the difference between average day and night temperatures is 14–17° F. Philadelphia is not in a desert, of course, and that is what makes the difference.

Water warms much more slowly than land and also cools more slowly. Water is said to have a high heat capacity, which means it requires a large amount of heat to raise its temperature. Heat capacity is the amount of heat required to raise the temperature of one gram of a substance by one kelvin (1 K =1° C). Pure water has

Adiabatic warming and cooling

Air is compressed by the weight of air above it. Imagine a balloon partly inflated with air and made from some substance that totally insulates the air inside. No matter what the temperature outside the balloon, the temperature of the air inside remains the same.

Imagine the balloon is released into the atmosphere. The air inside is squeezed between the weight of air above it, all the way to the top of the atmosphere, and the denser air below it.

Suppose the air inside the balloon is less dense than the air above it. The balloon will rise. As it rises, the distance to the top of the atmosphere becomes smaller, so there is less air above to weigh down on the air in the balloon. At the same time, as it moves through air that is less dense, it experiences less pressure from below. This causes the air in the balloon to expand.

When air (or any gas) expands, its molecules move further apart. The *amount* of air remains the same, but it occupies a bigger volume. As they move apart, the molecules must "push" other molecules out of their way. This uses energy, so as the air expands its molecules lose energy. Because they have less energy they move more slowly.

When a moving molecule strikes something, some of its energy of motion (kinetic energy) is transferred to whatever it strikes and part of that energy is converted into heat. This raises the temperature of the struck object by an amount related to the number of molecules striking it and their speed.

In expanding air, the molecules are moving further apart, so a smaller number of them strike an object each second. They are also traveling more slowly, so they strike with less force. This means the temperature of the air decreases. As it expands, air cools.

If the air in the balloon is denser than the air below, it will descend. The pressure on it will

Effect of air pressure on rising and sinking air.

increase, its volume will decrease, and its molecules will acquire more energy. Its temperature will increase.

This warming and cooling has nothing to do with the temperature of the air surrounding the balloon. It is called *adiabatic* warming and cooling, from the Greek word *adiabatos*, meaning impassable.

You can easily demonstrate adiabatic cooling and warming for yourself with experiment 1 described in *A Chronology of Weather*.

a heat capacity of 4.186 joules (1 calorie = 4.186 J) and that of sand is 0.8. In other words, it requires more than five times more heat to warm water through one degree than is required to warm sand by the same amount. During the day, therefore, water warms very slowly, but sand warms rapidly. At night, the sand cools rapidly, but water cools slowly. At Philadelphia the ground holds enough water to slow the rate at which it warms and cools and this reduces the difference between day and night temperatures. In a desert, where the ground holds little or no water, the difference in temperatures depends only on the heat capacity of sand and it is extreme. Deserts are hot by day, but can be very cold at night.

Even in a desert, there is water in some places. The Sahara is famous for its oases, lakes in the middle of the desert. Because there is water at the surface, oases support plants and animals. People live around them and farmers cultivate the land.

Oases are supplied by water that moves below ground (see page 55). There are two principal ways they can form, illustrated in figure 5. Even in a desert, when it rains heavily some of the water soaks into the ground before it can evaporate. It sinks through the sand and loose gravel that covers the desert surface until it reaches a layer of permeable rock, into which it soaks, above a layer of solid rock it cannot penetrate. There it accumulates as groundwater, flowing very slowly downhill through the porous material. Water may also enter from outside the desert. If the desert is in the rain shadow of mountains, for example, rain falling on the exposed side of the mountains may flow through them as groundwater and into the adjacent desert. Imagine the groundwater flowing over a large area, as a sheet of water possibly hundreds of miles wide, but deep below ground level.

Now suppose that in a certain place the wind has blown away surface sand and gravel. Over many years, the wind has hollowed

Figure 5: *What makes an oasis form.*

| | permeable rock | | impermeable rock | | water |

out the land, forming a deep depression. If this depression is deeper than the surface of the groundwater, water will flow through it and the depression will become a lake. Water will evaporate from the surface, of course, but it is constantly replenished from the groundwater, which also keeps the lake water fresh and wholesome, because on the downhill side of the lake the water continues its journey through the porous rock. The lake is permanent and the land around it is an oasis. This is the situation illustrated in the upper drawing of figure 5.

The lower drawing shows a different way an oasis can form. Here, groundwater flows through the porous rock as before, trapped above a layer of impermeable rock, but this time there is a fault in the rock layers. Movements of the Earth's crust have fractured the rocks and lifted those on the right (or lowered those on the left) of the drawing. Now the porous layer on the left ends where it meets impermeable rock. The water can flow no further, so it accumulates and its level rises until it meets the continuation of the porous layer on the right. Between the two, the water level rises to the surface and, once again, a permanent lake forms, as the center of an oasis.

Unfortunately, oases are few and far between and deserts are hostile places. There is very little water and temperatures fluctuate between extremes. Despite their climate, however, they support a surprisingly large amount of life.

Desert life

Walk out into the desert and you will see rock, gravel, dust, sand, and very little else. There may be no sign of anything living. The place is lifeless. Our word *desert* is from the Latin *desertus*, meaning forsaken. Without water nothing can live, and over most of the desert there is no water.

Nor can most plants and animals survive for long in very high temperatures. Photosynthesis is the process by which plants manufacture the carbohydrates that supply the energy they need to live and grow. Like all living organisms, they also respire. Respiration is the process by which carbohydrates are broken down to release energy. Plants, therefore, must strike a balance between their rates of photosynthesis and respiration. At temperatures above about 100° F, plants respire faster than they photosynthesize. Carbohydrates are being broken down in their tissues faster than they can be replaced, and so the plant starves. Very bright light makes the problem worse and desert plants are often exposed to high light intensity. At most light levels, the more intense the light a plant

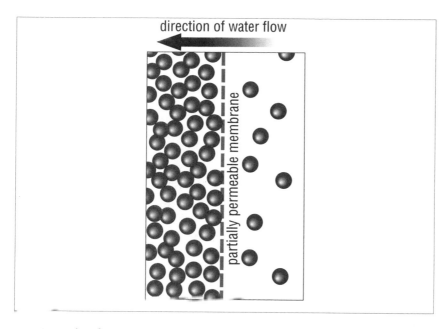

direction of water flow

partially permeable membrane

Figure 6: *Osmosis*.

receives the faster it photosynthesizes, but at very high intensities photosynthesis slows; the phenomenon is called *solarization*.

High temperatures can also damage enzymes, the proteins that regulate most of the chemistry of living organisms. If the enzymes are made inactive, or even destroyed, body chemistry is severely disrupted.

Water evaporates rapidly into hot, dry air, and the resulting loss of body fluids leads to dehydration. This is the most immediate and obvious danger to both plants and animals, and it conceals a vicious trap. Many organisms use the evaporation of water to keep cool. Humans do it when we sweat. This works, but the water must be replaced; otherwise, its loss leads to dehydration. The choice is between overheating or dehydrating.

Living cells are bounded by membranes through which certain molecules can pass. They are said to be partially permeable. If such a membrane separates two solutions, one much more concentrated than the other, the membrane will allow molecules of the solvent to pass, but hold back molecules of the solute (the dissolved substance). The solvent in our bodies, and those of plants and other animals, is water. When the body loses more water than it takes in, the concentration of dissolved substances increases in the fluid bathing its cells, and water flows out of the cells from the weaker to the stronger solution. This process is called *osmosis*, illustrated in figure 6. It continues until the solutions are at the same concentration on either side of the membrane. Its effect is to drain water from the cells until, in extreme cases, the cells no longer function normally and start to die. To compensate for this, water is drawn from the blood, which thickens until it ceases to flow fast enough to carry body heat to the skin where it can be lost, and the body temperature rises rapidly. That is why dehydration is so dangerous.

Facing such a formidable array of difficulties, it is not surprising that most organisms avoid deserts. For any plant or animal that can tolerate the harsh conditions, however, there are several important advantages. Deserts are not crowded, so there are plenty of places to find root or to nest, and the lack of competition means nutrients are abundant for those plants able to reach them. Seizing the opportunities is not easy, but some have managed to adapt, at least partially, and by no means is the desert so barren as it appears.

Avoidance or tolerance are the two survival strategies available to plants. Many choose avoidance. Some spend most of the time as seeds buried in the soil. Others are visible but appear to be dead. The seeds of some desert plants can remain buried for many years and then germinate as soon as they are moistened by rain. The ground will not remain moist for long and the plants must grow, flower, and produce a new crop of seeds before the drought returns. After it has rained, the apparently lifeless desert is briefly a mass of green plants and brightly colored flowers. *Boerhaavia repens*, a small African desert herb, may hold the record for a fast life cycle. It is said to take eight to ten days to germinate; mature; produce big, bright flowers pollinated by insects, and a crop of seeds. Then

Figure 7: *Some of the magnificent sand dunes near Sousevlei, Namibia, 1990.* (UN photo 157293/John Isaac)

it dies and disappears. Plant that appear and disappear rapidly in this way are called *ephemerals* and they waste no time growing elaborate roots. *Eschscholzia minutiflora*, a close relative of the Californian poppy, is a North American equivalent, but with tiny, yellow flowers rather than big ones.

Plants that appear to be dead may also be waiting for the rains. The ocotillo, or coachwhip (*Fouquieria splendens*) of North American deserts is typical. Most of the time it is a bunch of thin, unbranched stems, up to 15 feet tall, swaying in the wind. It has no leaves, but its stems are green and contain chlorophyll, so in fact the plant is photosynthesizing. When it rains, the ocotillo covers its stems in a mass of tiny leaves. These increase the area available for photosynthesis, allowing it to grow faster. When the rains cease and the air becomes dry, the leaves rapidly wither and fall. Each spring, buds develop at the tips of its stems and open as red flowers. Its close relative, the boojum tree (*Idria columnaris*) is very similar, but it grows as a single, thick, conical stem like an upside down carrot up to 60 feet tall, with a few branches and yellow flowers. The branches start erect, but they grow so long they often fall sideways under their own weight into weird shapes.

The boojum tree stores water in its carrot-like stem. Plants that do this are called *succulents* and the most famous examples are the *cacti*. Cacti are American plants, although they are now grown all over the world and have established themselves in the wild in many places. Their equivalents in the deserts of Africa, Asia, and Australia belong to the spurge family (Euphorbiaceae) and some of them closely resemble cacti.

Succulents have few, or in many species, no leaves. Instead, they have green stems in which photosynthesis takes place. The thick, fleshy stems store water. All plants have small pores, called *stomata*, through which they exchange gases with the atmosphere. This is essential. Plants need carbon dioxide for photosynthesis. Respiration provides some, but most of the time it is not enough. They can also use some of the oxygen, which is the byproduct of photosynthesis, for respiration, but not all of it, and the excess must be removed. Stomata are essential for exchange of other substances as well. Water vapor passes through them, and while its stomata are open a plant is losing water. This is not a problem for a plant that is rooted in moist soil from which its lost water can be replaced, but it might have serious consequences for a plant growing in arid desert soil. To make matters worse, if the temperature of the surface of the plant rises above that of the air next to it, the rate of evaporation from the open stomata increases sharply.

Desert plants deal with the problem in several ways. Some cacti have "ribs" and their stomata are confined to the "valleys" between them, where they are cooler from being shaded from direct sunlight. Other plants open their stomata early in the morning, then close them as the air grows warmer. Still others have very small leaves with an outer waxy coating that reduces evaporation.

This last method is adopted by possibly the most familiar plant of North American deserts, the creosote bush (*Larrea divaricata*). In addition to its small, waxy leaves, it is covered in hairs. These reflect light, which helps keep the plant cool. Its stomata are sunk into recesses in its leaves, and in very dry conditions the plant sheds its leaves altogether to conserve water. It also stores water in its tissues. The acacias of Africa are very similar and they are able to function efficiently at high temperatures. They photosynthesize best at 99° F, compared with 64° F for most plants of temperate climates.

Cacti, euphorbias, and acacias are often thorny or covered in spines that provide protection. A plant that stores water in its tissues cannot afford to lose it, and animals know there is water to be had if only they can break into the prickly plant.

Thorns, spines, and hairs also serve another purpose. Dew condenses on them at night, and this provides the plant with some water it can absorb. Welwitschia (*Welwitschia mirabilis*), one of the most remarkable of all plants, relies on collecting water from the air. It grows in the Namib Desert of southwest Africa. It has only two leaves, which curl and are split into straps by the wind. They grow continuously, but wear away at their ends. Even so, their total surface area amounts to about 25 square yards. The leaves collect dew and also moisture from sea mists that roll up to 50 miles inland from the South Atlantic. The welwitschia does everything slowly. When one of its seeds germinates, the seed leaves (cotyledons) last for five years before true leaves appear, during which time the plant grows a taproot up to 60 feet deep. The plant itself lives for up to 2,000 years. There are also animals that obtain moisture from the mists over the Namib. At dawn, beetles stand on top of sand dunes with their abdomens raised. The beetles have cooled during the night and water condenses on their bodies and trickles down to their mouths.

All animals obtain some water from the food they eat, even if the food is very dry. This is not water contained in the food, but a byproduct of respiration. When carbohydrates are oxidized to release energy (which is what respiration means) water is one of the products. The general equation is: carbohydrate + oxygen → carbon dioxide + water + energy. This water is removed from the body along with the carbon dioxide. It is what condenses when you breathe on a cold mirror or windowpane. In the desert, animals cannot afford to waste water. Some, like the kangaroo rat, spend much of their time below ground, which is also where they store their food. As they breathe, their store of dry plant material absorbs moisture from their breath, so they recover it whenever they eat.

Kangaroo rats never need to drink and all desert animals must be able to survive a long time without drinking. Many of the small mammals have noses that cool their breath before it leaves their bodies, so water condenses from it and is absorbed, and most desert animals excrete a very concentrated urine from which most of the water has been removed. A camel loses less than two pints of water a day in its urine and it does not start sweating until its temperature exceeds 100° F. The skins of reptiles and scorpions are almost completely impermeable, so no water can be lost by that route.

Walk barefoot over sand on a very hot day and the sand will burn your feet, but the skin on your head does not burn. It is at ground level that the temperature is highest. Just a few feet higher or lower the air is much cooler. A camel stands about 8 feet tall to the top of its hump and the midday temperature there may be 60° F lower than the temperature at ground level. Even a short distance helps. Some lizards climb into bushes, where the air is cooler, and others, such as *Palmatogecko rangei*, a gecko that lives in the Kalahari, stand with one foot raised, from time to time replacing one foot and raising another.

Five feet below ground, where many small animals rest during the hottest part of the day, the temperature may be as much as 80° F lower than that at the surface. Animals that do a great deal of burrowing through loose sand have become very good at it. Some lizards and snakes swim just below the surface, and so does Grant's desert mole (*Eremitalpa granti*) of the Namib Desert. It has no eyes or external ears, but despite this apparent handicap is a successful underground hunter of insects and lizards sheltering from the heat. Many burrowers have big feet to help with the shoveling, but skinks, a group of lizards with small legs and, in some species, no legs at all, manage differently. They hold their little legs to the sides of their bodies as they swim through the sand, like fish.

Some burrowers dive headfirst into the sand. Many lizards with triangular heads vanish this way. Others use a sideways movement, pushing sand away to make a trench into which they sink until they are deep enough for the loose sand to fall back and cover them.

Once below ground, an animal is invisible. This makes burrowing a good way to hide from enemies, but it is also a good way to hide while waiting for prey or even while searching for it. The sidewinder rattlesnake (*Crotalus cerastes*) and the horned viper (*Cerastes cerastes*) are among several species of desert snakes that hunt in this way. They have short, thick bodies, can spread their ribs to flatten themselves, are covered in scales that give a good grip on loose sand, and their raised eyes are protected by horns. These snakes shuffle along below the surface with just their eyes above ground. Sand boas of western Asia are similar in overall design, but are constrictors rather than venomous snakes.

Sidewinders are best known for their curious method of locomotion. This works well on soft ground, but place them on a firm surface and they move like any other snake, and place most snakes on soft sand and they will make an attempt at sidewinding.

Unrelated plants and animals living in areas thousands of miles apart often come to resemble one another. This is called *convergent evolution* and it arises when the same solution to a particular problem appears more than once. Extreme environments provide many examples, none more than deserts. The cacti of America are very similar to some of the euphorbias of Africa and Asia; for example, the American creosote bush looks much like an African acacia, and among animals the similarities are even more striking. The greatest exponents of sidewinding are the American sidewinder rattlesnake, the horned viper and carpet viper (*Echis carinatus*) of North Africa and the Middle East, and *Bitis peringueyi*, a South African viper. The 70 or so species of American kangaroo rats (genus *Dipodomys*) live in a similar way and look very like the jerboas (genus *Jaculus*) of the Sahara and Arabian Deserts. In the North American desert you may see a kit fox (*Vulpes velox*), a delicate animal with very large ears. Blood vessels passing through the thin cartilage of the ears carry heat away from the body, so big ears help an animal keep cool. In the Sahara the fennec (*Fennecus zerda*) is another fox that also has big ears.

The list is long and the reason simple. Desert life is hard and there are only a few ways a plant or animal can keep cool and save water. It is not surprising that identical solutions have evolved in widely separated places.

Polar deserts

When Captain Robert Scott crossed Antarctica in 1903 in his first attempt to reach the South Pole, to his surprise he and his party came across a sheltered valley. No snow or ice was to be seen, and the sand on the valley floor felt warm as he trickled it through his fingers. What the expedition had found was one of several "dry valleys." Together they occupy about 2,200 square miles. This is a tiny fraction of the 5,400,000 square miles that is the area of the entire continent, but they are interesting. Very little lives there. Scott saw no sign of life, although there are bacteria and a few mosses and lichens. In fact, apart from their much lower temperature they are very similar to the dry deserts found elsewhere, despite being surrounded by vast amounts of snow and ice. They are dry partly because the small amount of snow that falls on them is swept away by winds that exceed 100 MPH, and partly because their dark-colored rocks and sand absorb enough warmth from the Sun to melt any snow that does settle.

Most of Antarctica lies beneath ice. The thickness of ice varies greatly from place to place, but on average the ice sheet is almost 7,000 feet thick. Around 90% of all the ice in the world is in Antartica. There is even liquid water in the form of at least 70 freshwater lakes beneath the ice sheet. These are kept liquid by heat from the radioactive decay of elements in the underlying rock (the main source of heat in Earth's crust) and insulated by the thick layer of ice above them. The discovery of what may be the largest was announced in June 1996. Lake Vostok, lying beneath more than 13,000 feet of ice near the Russian Vostok station (at about 78° S), is about 125 miles long, covering an area of 5,400 square miles, and in places it is more than 1,500 feet deep. The continent is not short of water. Indeed, it contains about 95% of all the fresh water in the world.

If you visit Antarctica by sea there is a good chance you will sail through some very bad weather. You will pass through latitudes sailors rounding the southern tips of South America and Africa called the "roaring forties," "furious fifties," and "shrieking sixties." As their names suggest, the gales intensify the farther south you go.

You will also cross the polar front, where tropical air to the north meets polar air to the south, in summer at about 45° S and in winter rather father to the north. This front produces violent storms that lash the coast. Heavy snow and blizzards are common, but in summer there are long spells of clear weather. When you arrive, assuming the weather then is fine, you will be greeted by spectacular scenery sculpted entirely from ice.

What with the fierce snowstorms, the huge icebergs your ship will have passed, and the landscape of endless snow, you may well conclude that Antarctica has a wet climate. Indeed, that does describe the part of it you will have seen, where the annual precipitation is about 15 inches, but Antarctica is a big continent and the coastal weather does not travel far inland. In its deep interior it is desert, and possibly the driest desert in the world.

Apart from the dry valleys, the land is everywhere covered by ice, but this does not mean the climate is moist. It is too cold for the ice to melt even in summer and the Antarctic climate has been like this for many millions of years. When snow falls it adds to what has fallen before and the ice sheet is the result of a very long, very slow accumulation.

Measuring snowfall is difficult under Antarctic conditions. The snow itself is usually fine and powdery. It blows easily, and the winds are always strong and have been known to blow at 200 MPH. They tend to blow the snow across the snow gauges rather than letting it fall into them, and when the snowfall ends there is no way of distinguishing what has just fallen from the snow onto which it fell. Even if that were possible, the wind drives the snow into drifts, so its thickness varies widely. To allow for the many different kinds

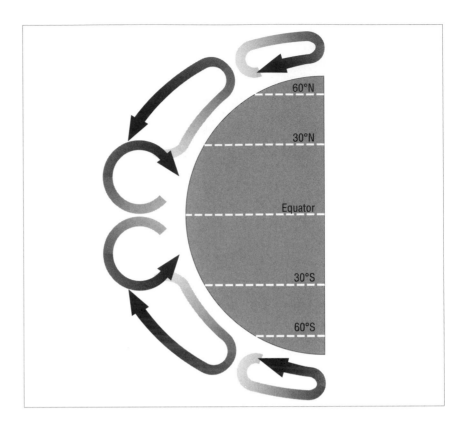

Figure 8: *Global circulation of the atmosphere.*

of snow, measurements of snowfall are usually converted into the equivalent amount of rainfall. The interior of Antarctica probably receives an average of little more than two inches of rainfall-equivalent a year. Regardless of temperature, if the annual rainfall is less than 10 inches the land is likely to be a desert. So Antarctica is a desert.

Greenland also lies beneath an ice sheet. Its average thickness is about 5,000 feet. Thule, in the north at latitude 76.5°, receives about 2.5 inches of precipitation a year, well below the 10-inch threshold. The equation $r \div (t + 14)$ gives a value of 2.2 (see page 11). This is more than 1, but nevertheless indicates a dry climate, and Thule is on the coast. The climate of Thule is believed to be typical of that over most of the interior, but probably moister because of its coastal location. More rain and snow fall further south but, like the interior of Antarctica, northern Greenland and much of the interior is a dry desert situated on top of an ice sheet.

Over both poles, cold, dense air is subsiding, much as it does over the deserts in low latitudes. This movement is part of the global circulation of the atmosphere, illustrated in figure 8 by which warm air moves from the equator towards the poles and cool air moves from the poles to the equator.

The circulation pattern that makes polar regions dry deserts begins with the tropical Hadley cells (see page 8). It is subsiding air from the Hadley cells that produces deserts at around latitude 30° in both hemispheres, but not all the air sinks into the subtropics. Some continues to move away from the equator, all the way to the poles. Near the surface, some of the air subsiding into the subtropics returns to the equator, but some turns the other way, heading toward the poles. When air reaches the poles it can travel no further because it meets air that is also traveling poleward from all around the world. Air accumulates and becomes dense enough to sink. This is what generates the subsiding air over the central arctic and antarctic regions. At the surface, the air has no choice but to flow away from the poles until, at around latitude 60° in both hemispheres, it meets air moving away from the tropical Hadley cells. The converging air rises and joins the high-level flow, some of the air moving towards the pole and some towards the equator.

In reality, the air movements are more complicated, but this general description is called the "three-cell model" of atmospheric circulation. The first cell is the tropical Hadley cell. The second is the polar cell, of subsiding air over the pole and rising air at about 60°. These two cells drive the third, midlatitude cell.

Just as the geographic equator does not coincide with the climatic equator (see page 7), so the climatic poles are not in precisely the same place as the geographic poles. This makes little difference at the South Pole, where the two are close together, but the two North Poles are a long way apart. The climatic North Pole, often called the "cold pole," is close to Verkhoyansk in Siberia, at 65° N 133.5° E. This and Oimyakon, a small town about 300 miles to the southeast, are the coldest places in the northern hemisphere, with an average January temperature of −58° F that can fall as low as − 90° F. The South Pole is colder. In winter, the temperature can fall below −125° F. Unlike central Antarctica, Verkhoyansk is not cold all year round. In July the average temperature is 56° F, but it has been known to exceed 90° F.

Like the area around the South Pole, Verkhoyansk has a dry climate. Its annual rainfall averages 5 inches, falling mainly in summer. The average temperature is −17° C and $r \div (t + 14) = -4.5$. This is less than 1, so Verkhoyansk lies within a very dry desert.

Relative humidity (RH) at Verkhoyansk ranges from 45–78% during the day, but at night it sometimes exceeds 80%. This makes it sound as though the climate should be wetter than it is, but remember that as the temperature falls the relative humidity rises, because cold air can hold less water vapor than warm air. In May, when the average daytime temperature is 43° F, the average RH is 47%; if the temperature were 68° F the same amount of atmospheric moisture would give an RH of 19%.

It may seem that the problems of survival are quite different in the polar deserts from those in a subtropical desert, but in fact they are very similar. It is true that in Antarctica and Greenland there is no shortage of water, but water is abundant there only for humans. We can light fires and melt the ice. Plants cannot do that, and it is only as a liquid that their roots can absorb water, without which they die (see page 51). Frozen water is not available to them, so as far as plants are concerned frozen ground is no different from completely arid ground. Predictably, very few plants grow in the polar deserts. Despite the hostility of the climate, in dry valleys and on mountainsides, where bare rock and sand are exposed, mosses and lichens are able to grow for a few days in summer, when the dark-colored surface absorbs enough heat to melt a little water for them. In sheltered places, the absorption of sunlight in midsummer, when daylight is almost continuous, can briefly raise the temperature of rocks to more than 80° F. For the rest of the year these simple plants remain dormant.

Mammals might be able to melt ice with the warmth of their bodies, but all animals need food and all food is obtained in the first instance from plants. Meat-eaters may consume no plants, but they eat plant-eaters, which do. With so few plants, polar deserts are even more devoid of animal life than hot deserts.

Low-latitude deserts are hot during the day and much cooler, or even cold, at night. It is almost never hot in a polar desert, but temperature is no less of a problem. Plants can adapt to limited periods of very low temperatures, but photosynthesis ceases below about 20° F. If respiration continues, the plants will "starve," just as plants do at very high temperatures (see page 14).

Polar deserts are as dry as the more familiar subtropical deserts and conditions in them are, if anything, even harsher. Compared with them, the hot deserts of America, Africa, Asia, and Australia are teeming with life.

Precipitation, evaporation, sublimation, and ablation

Imagine it is early in the winter and you are outdoors looking at a small lake. Ice has begun to form around the edges of the lake and now covers part of the surface. You can see ice and liquid water and the air around you contains water vapor. Water is present in its solid, liquid, and gaseous forms, all in the same place at the same time.

The vapor is invisible, of course, but it is there all the same. Air always contains some water vapor. In really dry weather you might think the air was as dry as the ground, but even then there is moisture in the air and there is even some in the soil that seems completely dry. If you doubt it, wait until a day when you think the air and ground are really dry and try experiment 25 in *A Chronology of Weather.*

Water is the only common substance that can exist in all three states at ordinary temperatures. We take it for granted and everyone knows that water freezes at 32° F and boils at 212° F (though this is true only of pure water at sea-level atmospheric pressure; impurities and changes in pressure alter its freezing and boiling points).

Commonplace it may be, but this property of water is remarkable. You can calculate the freezing and melting points of substances from the size of their molecules. Water molecules, comprising two atoms of hydrogen and one of oxygen (H_2O), are much the same size as those of ammonia (NH_3), hydrochloric acid (HCl), and methane (CH_4), but water freezes and boils at much higher temperatures than any of these. The freezing and boiling points of ammonia are −108° F and −28° F; of hydrochloric acid −175° F and −121° F; and of methane −299° F and −263° F.

It is not the size of its molecules that gives water its peculiar properties, but their composition and structure. Each molecule

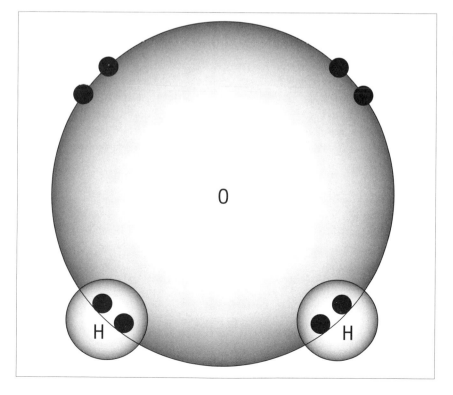

Figure 9: *Position of outer-shell electrons in a water molecule.*

consists of an atom of oxygen bonded to two hydrogen atoms, both of which are on the same side of the oxygen atom, separated by an angle of 104.5°. The water molecule is shaped like a rather open V and its atoms are held together by attraction between opposite electrical charges. Figure 9 shows how this works. The nucleus of each atom carries a positive charge, which is balanced by the negative charge of its electrons. The atoms in a water molecule share some of their outermost electrons. This is called a *covalent* bond. It leaves four of the oxygen electrons (negative charge) on the oxygen side of the molecule and the four shared with hydrogen atoms balancing the positive charge on the oxygen nucleus, but not the whole of the charge on the two hydrogen nuclei. The result is a small negative charge at the oxygen end of the molecule and a small positive charge at the hydrogen end.

When hydrogen forms a molecule with oxygen, fluorine, or nitrogen, each of which carries a strongly negative charge, a further bond can form between the hydrogen in the molecule and the negatively charged atom in another molecule. This is called a hydrogen bond, and it links water molecules together as groups of molecules in the liquid and more firmly in ice.

Molecules are in constant motion, and the more energy they have the faster they move and the greater the distance between them. In a gas, the molecules move independently of one another, in straight lines, ricocheting when they collide with one another or any other object. Cool them and they lose energy, move closer together, and become a liquid. At still lower temperatures they lock together so tightly they can only vibrate, and form a solid. In order to change from solid to liquid or liquid to gas, the molecules must absorb enough energy to accelerate them to the required speed. In most cases, the energy this requires depends on the size of the molecules, but if molecules in the liquid and solid are linked by hydrogen bonds additional energy is needed to break those bonds. This raises the melting and boiling points of substances with hydrogen bonds. Ammonia and water molecules are linked by hydrogen bonds and without them would melt and boil at lower temperatures.

The energy needed to break the attraction between molecules has no effect on the temperature of the substance. It is called *latent heat* and, because of its hydrogen bonds, the latent heat of water is higher than that of most substances. For pure water, 600 calories of energy must be absorbed to change one gram (1 g = 0.035 oz.) from liquid to gas (evaporation) and 80 calories to melt one gram of ice. Sublimation, which is the direct change between ice and vapor without passing through the liquid phase, absorbs 680 calories for each gram (the sum of the latent heats of melting and evaporation). When these changes proceed in the opposite direction, as water vapor condenses and liquid water freezes, the same amount of latent heat is released as the hydrogen bonds form. This means that although the absorption and release of latent heat does not change the temperature of the water, it does affect the temperature of its surroundings, because it is from its surroundings that latent heat must be taken and into them that it must be released.

At 212° F pure water boils, but it will evaporate at any temperature. Within the liquid, all the molecules are moving, the hydrogen bonds that link them into small groups constantly breaking and reforming; the warmer the water the faster the molecules move. If you heat water, the heat is absorbed by individual molecules. This addition of energy accelerates them and some move fast enough to break from the surface. If they enter air that already contains so much water vapor it can hold no more, vapor molecules condense onto the water surface. So over the surface of water, molecules are leaping into the air and condensing back into the liquid all the time, but some of the water molecules escape from this surface layer into the air beyond. That is evaporation.

In very cold but sunny weather, when the temperature is well below freezing, thin patches of snow and ice sometimes dwindle in size and eventually disappear. The ice has evaporated directly into the air. This is called *sublimation*. Water molecules in the ice or snow crystals have absorbed enough energy from the sunshine for them to break their hydrogen bonds and escape. This requires more energy than the escape from liquid, because there are more hydrogen bonds linking the molecules in ice. The air must also be very dry, because at low temperatures it can hold only a little water vapor.

Glaciers and snowfields also lose snow and ice, even in the coldest conditions, by a combination of melting and sublimation. The overall effect is called *ablation*, and the rate at which it occurs depends on the air temperature, humidity, the intensity of the sunshine and various other factors.

One of these is the wind. Water evaporates or sublimes much more readily in a wind than when the air is still and the stronger the wind the faster it carries away water vapor. We have been making use of this throughout history, of course, every time we have hung out washing to dry in the wind. It happens because of air turbulence. As the wind blows across a surface, small irregularities produce eddies. These carry much of the water vapor aloft and replace it at the surface with dry air from a higher level, into which more water can evaporate or sublime.

Once airborne, water vapor may be carried in air that cools to a temperature at which it becomes saturated and the vapor starts to condense into droplets (see box on page 28). This is called its *dew-point temperature* and experiment 11 in volume 6 explains how you can measure it.

Evaporation, condensation, and the formation of clouds

When air rises it cools adiabatically, by an average of 5.5° F every 1,000 feet. This is called the *dry adiabatic lapse rate*. Moving air may be forced to rise if it crosses high ground, such as a mountain or mountain range, or meets a mass of cooler, denser air at a front. Locally, air may also rise by convection where the ground is warmed unevenly.

There will be a height, called the *condensation level*, at which the temperature of the air falls to its dew point. As the air rises above this level the water vapor it contains will start to condense. Condensation releases latent heat, warming the air. After the relative humidity of the air reaches 100% and the air continues to rise, it will cool at the saturated adiabatic lapse rate of about 3° F per 1,000 feet.

Water vapor will condense at a relative humidity as low as 78% if the air contains minute particles of a substance that readily dissolves in water. Salt crystals and sulfate particles are common examples. Such substances readily take up water molecules from the air and become droplets of a concentrated solution. Water evaporates much more slowly from a solution than from pure water, so the droplets survive longer and grow by gathering more water molecules. If the air contains insoluble particles, such as dust, the vapor will condense at about 100% relative humidity. If there are no particles at all, the relative humidity may exceed 100% and the air will be supersaturated, although the relative humidity in clouds rarely exceeds 101%.

The particles onto which water vapor condenses are called *cloud condensation nuclei* (CCN). They range in size from 0.001 μm to more than 10 μm in diameter; water will condense onto the smallest particles only if the air is strongly supersaturated, and the largest particles are so heavy they do not remain airborne very long. Condensation is most efficient on CCN averaging 0.2 μm diameter (1 μm = one-millionth of a meter = 0.00004 inches).

At first, water droplets vary in size according to the size of the nuclei on to which they condensed. After that, the droplets grow but also lose water by evaporation because they are warmed by the latent heat of condensation. Some freeze, grow into snowflakes, and then melt as they fall into a lower, warmer region of the cloud. Others grow as large droplets collide and merge with smaller ones.

Cloud Formation.
  1) forced to rise over high ground (orographic lifting)
  2) convection due to uneven heating of the ground
  3) forced to rise along a front

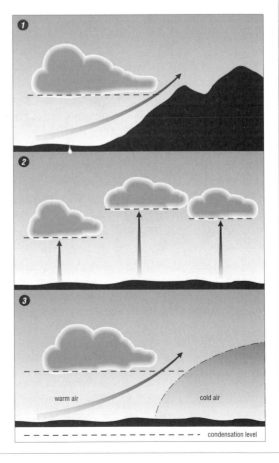

During a drought, water continues to evaporate, but often without condensing again. The air is so dry it can hold all the water vapor entering it without becoming saturated. Even if clouds form, no rain falls from them.

Watch the puffs of white cloud that drift across the sky on a fine day and they look quite stable. Study them through binoculars, however, and you will see they are constantly changing. Small bulges and wisps appear from them constantly, only to vanish a few moments later, and the whole cloud may last no more than a few hours before all its water evaporates. It may take no more than half an hour for one of these little clouds to grow into a huge storm cloud seven miles tall and six miles across, and yet an hour later that great cloud can have disappeared completely. Even in extremely cloudy weather, when a solid sheet of cloud covers the entire sky for days on end, individual parts of the cloud may last no more than a day or two. Air moves through the cloud so fast it soon carries bits of cloud away from the main mass and into drier air, where its droplets evaporate. Inside any cloud the individual water droplets and ice crystals last much less than an hour before they evaporate or sublime.

Clouds are very dynamic. Their water is constantly evaporating and condensing again, but some droplets and ice crystals manage to remain in a liquid or solid state. To achieve this they must reach a certain size. They can do this only if the air immediately around them is slightly supersaturated (its relative humidity is greater than 100%). This prevent their molecules from escaping as vapor, and if air movements around them can bring more water vapor to them and carry away the latent heat of condensation, the droplets will grow. They start very small, no more than about 0.2 μm (0.000008 inch) in diameter, but once they start to grow their size increases very rapidly. As soon as the droplets are more than about 100 μm (0.04 inch) across they start to fall. As they fall, they collide and merge with other droplets. When they are more than 200 μm (0.08 inch) in diameter they are heavy enough to fall from clouds in which there are only very weak upcurrents of air. If they reach the ground, they are drizzle.

Droplets grow this way only in warm clouds, however, and most clouds are cold, even in the middle of summer and even over a hot desert. If the temperature at ground level is 90° F, it will be 30° F at 11,000 feet if air temperature decreases with height at the dry adiabatic lapse rate (see box). Where the temperature is below freezing, supercooled water vapor will not condense into droplets, but will sublime directly into ice crystals. Once this process begins it proceeds much faster than the condensation of vapor into liquid droplets. The cloud may then contain ice crystals near the top and water droplets in the lower levels, which are warmer. Ice crystals falling through the cold layers will grow as more supercooled droplets freeze onto them, but when they reach levels where the temperature is a degree or two above freezing they start to melt. In most clouds, even over the equator, droplets grow by a mixture of freezing and the growth of ice crystals and the collision and merging of water droplets.

Eventually, when they are heavy enough, droplets fall from the base of the cloud. In fact, though, much smaller droplets are leaving the cloud all the time. The bulges and wisps that appear only to vanish again all around the fine-weather cloud you examine with binoculars are made from water droplets or, near the top of a tall cloud, ice crystals. After they emerge from the main mass of the cloud they do not disappear because they have returned into it. They evaporate. Water vapor condenses because the relative humidity reaches saturation, but this does not happen everywhere. Where it does, cloud forms and where it does not the air remains clear. Droplets that leave the cloud enter unsaturated air and simply evaporate, ice crystals sublime. That is why clouds have shapes and why they also have clearly defined bases.

The air between the base of a cloud and the ground is not saturated. If it were, water vapor would condense in it and the cloud would extend to ground level, as fog. This means water falling from the cloud enters unsaturated air and immediately starts to evaporate. Only drops of more than a certain minimum size can reach the ground before they vaporize.

The bigger the droplets, the greater their mass in relation to their surface area. If the droplet is spherical, with a diameter of, say, 2 units, its volume ($4/3\ \pi r^3$) will be 4.18 and its surface area ($4\pi r^2$) 12.6; if its diameter is 4 units its volume will be 33.5 and its surface area 50.3. The ratio of volume to surface area for the first is 1:3.0 and for the second 1:1.5. Having a smaller surface area in relation to its weight (or mass), the bigger droplet will encounter relatively less air resistance than the smaller one, so it will fall faster. A drizzle droplet 200 μm in diameter falls at about 2.5 feet per second and a rain droplet 500 μm in diameter falls at about 13 feet per second. Not only does the bigger droplet contain more water, allowing it to survive longer before it vaporizes, it also falls faster, so it spends less time in the air.

Even so, the rain may never reach the ground. During a drought, and over a desert, the relative humidity of the air is low. The condensation level, marking the cloud base, will be fairly high and water falling from the cloud will have to travel a considerable distance through extremely dry air. Clouds do appear, over even the driest deserts, and some of them may be big enough to produce rain, but the rain evaporates in the dry air just below the cloud. Only towering storm clouds can release water fast enough to saturate the air beneath the cloud as drops evaporate and allow those which follow to fall to the ground.

Ocean currents and sea-surface temperature

Sunshine warms the ground and the ground warms the air in contact with it. At the equator, the warm air rises and moves away to north and south. Thus begins the circulation of the atmosphere by which heat is carried from the equator to the poles. Without it, tropical climates would be very much hotter than they are, and polar climates very much colder.

It is only part of the story, however, for the Sun shines on both land and sea, and unlike the rocks and soil of the land, the waters of the sea can move. Their movements also carry warmth from low to high latitudes, but the patterns the waters make are rather different from those of air movements. There is no oceanic equivalent of the tropical Hadley cells and the other two systems of atmospheric cells (see page 8).

The outcome is similar. Water is warmed near the equator, moves north and south, and its place is taken by cooler water flowing in from higher latitudes. In each of the major oceans (North and South Atlantic, North and South Pacific, and Indian) water moves as currents flowing clockwise in the northern hemisphere and counterclockwise in the southern. These major currents are called *gyres* and they follow approximately circular paths because of the combined effects of prevailing winds; the Coriolis effect, which deflects bodies moving away from the equator (see box on page 32); vorticity, which is the tendency of all moving liquids and gases to rotate about a vertical axis; and the Ekman effect. This was first observed in 1905 by the Swedish oceanographer V. W. Ekman (see *A Chronology of Weather* for more details). By tracking the movement of sea ice carried by wind-driven ocean currents he found that the currents follows paths about 45° to the right of the wind direction. This is due to friction between water moving at different speeds, and the angle of deflection increases with depth, in what is called an *Ekman spiral*, down to an *Ekman depth* at which the current is flowing in the opposite direction to the surface current.

To either side of the equator, the trade winds blowing from the northeast in the northern hemisphere and southeast in the southern drive currents flowing from east to west. These are the North and South Equatorial Currents. In the North Atlantic, the North Equatorial Current turns northward (to the right) as it approaches North America, becoming in turn the Antilles and Florida Currents and then the Gulf Stream, which flows along the North American coast,

The Coriolis effect

Any object moving towards or away from the equator and not firmly attached to the surface does not travel in a straight line. It is deflected to the right in the northern hemisphere and to the left in the southern hemisphere. Moving air and water tend to follow a clockwise path in the northern hemisphere and a counterclockwise path in the southern hemisphere.

The reason for this was discovered in 1835 by the French physicist Gaspard Gustave de Coriolis and it is called the *Coriolis effect*. It happens because the Earth is a rotating sphere and as an object moves above the surface, the Earth below is also moving. The effect used to be called the Coriolis *force*, but it is not a force.

It results simply from the fact that we observe motion in relation to fixed points on the surface. The effect is easily demonstrated by the simple experiment described in volume 6.

The Earth makes one complete turn on its axis every 24 hours. This means every point on the surface is constantly moving and returns to its original position (relative to the Sun) every 24 hours, but different points on the surface travel different distances to do so. Consider two points on the surface, one at the equator and the other at 40° N, which is the approximate latitude of New York and Madrid. The equator, latitude 0°, is about 24,881 miles long. That is how far a point on the equator

The Coriolis effect.

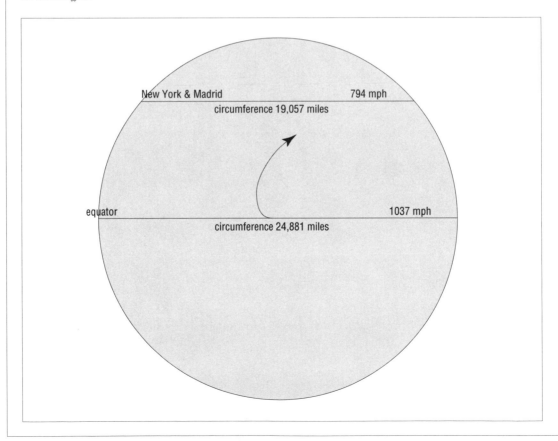

New York & Madrid   794 mph
circumference 19,057 miles

equator   1037 mph
circumference 24,881 miles

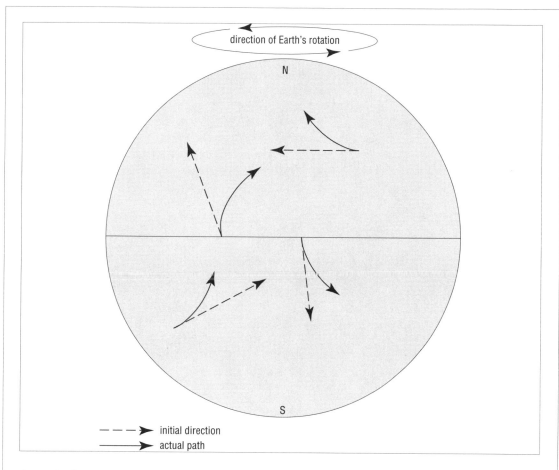

direction of Earth's rotation

N

S

- - - ▸ initial direction
———▸ actual path

The Coriolis effect: The Coriolis effect deflects air masses and winds to the right in the northern hemisphere and to the left in the southern hemisphere. It has no effect at the equator and maximum effect at the poles.

must travel in 24 hours, which means it moves at about 1,037 MPH. At 40° N, the circumference parallel to the equator is about 19,057 miles. The point there has less distance to travel and so it moves at about 794 MPH.

Suppose you planned to fly an aircraft to New York from the point on the equator due south of New York (and could ignore the winds). If you headed due north you would not reach New York. At the Equator you are already traveling eastward at 1,037 MPH. As you fly north, the surface beneath you is also traveling east, but at a slower speed the further you travel. If the journey from 0° to 40° N took you 6 hours,

in that time you would also move about 6,000 miles to the east relative to the position of the surface beneath you, but the surface itself would also move, at New York by about 4,700 miles, so you would end not at New York, but (6,000 − 4,700 =) 1,300 miles to the east of New York, way out over the Atlantic.

The size of the Coriolis effect is directly proportional to the speed at which the body moves and the sine of its latitude. The effect on a body moving at 100 MPH is ten times greater than that on one moving at 10 MPH, and the Coriolis effect is greatest at the poles and zero at the equator.

out into the Atlantic, and turns south in the latitude of Portugal and Spain to rejoin the North Equatorial Current. As it starts to turn south, however, part of it breaks away as the North Atlantic Drift. This current washes the coasts of northwest Europe and becomes the Norwegian Current as it passes the coast of Norway into the Arctic Ocean. A current also flows northward along the west coast of Greenland and south, as the Labrador Current, along the Canadian east coast. It meets the Gulf Stream near Newfoundland, where the reaction between warm and cold water generates frequent fogs.

The South Equatorial Current in the Atlantic flows as the Brazil Current down the east coast of South America all the way to the Antarctic Circle, where it joins the West Wind Drift, a current flowing from west to east right around Antarctica, but with a branch flowing north along the west coast of Africa as the Benguela Current.

In the Pacific, the Kuroshio and Oyashio Currents flow northward along the Japanese and mainland Asian coasts and the California Current flows south along the west coast of North America. To the south, the East Australia Current flows down the east coast of Australia and into the West Wind Drift, and the Peru (or Humboldt) Current flows north along the west coast of South America.

Winds are the principal force driving ocean currents, but they are not the only one. In the North Atlantic, near the edge of the Arctic sea ice, dense water sinks beneath less dense water to its south, forming the North Atlantic Deep Water (NADW) that flows close to the floor of the Atlantic all the way to Antarctica.

Two factors, salinity and temperature, combine to increase the density of the water adjacent to the sea ice and cause it to sink to become the NADW. Common salt is sodium chloride (NaCl). Its sodium atom carries a positive electrical charge (written as Na^+) and its chlorine atom a negative charge (Cl^-). As figure 10 shows, when salt dissolves in water its sodium and chlorine separate. The sodium is attracted to the oxygen end of the water molecules (0^-) and its chlorine to the hydrogen end (H^+). When the water freezes, its molecules move closer together and the sodium and chlorine are ejected, so ice consists of fresh water. Experiment 14 in volume 6 lets you demonstrate this for yourself. The ejected salt goes into the water that is still unfrozen and, because that water now contains more salt, the density of the more salty solution increases. At the same time, the water near the edge of the ice is very cold, but not quite at freezing temperature. Water reaches its greatest density at about 39° F, which is the approximate temperature of the chilled water.

The water sinking to become the NADW is replaced at the surface by warmer water flowing north and this mechanism accounts for the North Atlantic Drift and contributes to the entire circulation of the Atlantic. Scientists believe changes in the formation of NADW, leading to changes in the ocean circulation, have been responsible

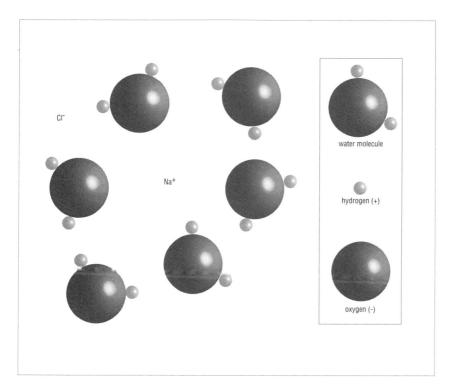

Figure 10: *Common salt (NaCl) in solution.*

for major changes in climate in the past. Should the formation of NADW change again in years to come, this would have a large effect on climate (see page 121).

In general, the ocean circulation brings warm water to the eastern coasts of continents and cool water to the western coasts. Its direct climatic effect is small, but significant, because coasts washed by warm currents enjoy milder winters than those washed by cold currents. More importantly, the current system carries warm water into high latitudes and thus contributes to the overall transport of heat.

The North Atlantic Drift and Norwegian Current are the exception to the general rule, because they bring warm water to northwest Europe. This does influence the climate. At Vancouver, for example, the average daytime temperature in January is 41° F and in Cherbourg, France, also on a west coast and in the same latitude, it is 47° F, but whereas the lowest January temperature recorded in Vancouver is 2° F, in Cherbourg it is 21° F. Poolewe, in a sheltered location on the west coast of Scotland at 57° 46' N, is especially favored. A garden there contains plants more typical of a Mediterranean climate. Poolewe is in the same latitude as Kodiak Island, Alaska!

Scientists still have much to learn about the influence of ocean currents on climates, but there is no doubt that it is considerable.

El Niño and La Niña

Irregularly, at intervals of two to seven years, climates all over the world are affected by a change in the circulation of air and an associated change in a particular ocean current. The effects of these events are so widespread and often dramatic as to provide a clear demonstration of the extent to which our weather systems are linked to the transport of heat by the oceans. Ordinarily this is not easy to see. Like some obscure component of a car engine, it is only when it goes wrong that we become aware of its existence. In fact, it is not even that obvious. When part of an engine fails, the engine refuses to work normally and usually stops altogether. In this case, people simply assumed that unusual weather would happen from time to time and did not think too hard about what might be causing it.

The effects were recorded, but it is only quite recently that scientists have discovered the reason for them. The change in an ocean current linked to the effects was known, but until the middle 1970s this change was thought to be much too small to be of much importance, except very locally, perhaps. Then, in 1976, it was linked to drought, famine, and the collapse of one of most important fisheries in the world, all of which had taken place in 1972 and 1973. After that, the scientific investigation of the phenomenon accelerated and much more has been learned about it.

The first reported instance of this particular change in the weather is believed to have been in 1541. Clearly it is not a new phenomenon and probably it has been happening every few years for thousands of years. More recently, it has occurred on a large scale in 1925, 1941, 1957, 1965, 1972, 1982, and 1987. It was also recorded in 1992 and 1995, but more detailed studies revealed that a single episode began in 1990 and continued until the middle of 1995.

Despite having been overlooked for so many years, what is now regarded as the first clue to what happens was discovered in 1923. Sir Gilbert Walker, a British meteorologist who had been director of the Indian meteorological service since 1904, had a particular interest in the causes of the Asian monsoons, and because they are so important to farmers in the subcontinent, in why they are weak or fail entirely in some years. Monsoon failures had caused severe famine in Indian in 1877 and 1899. The mechanism is quite complex (see page 86) and the studies Walker started have advanced greatly since his time, but he did find that the easterly trade winds are balanced by a westerly (west to east) airflow close to the tropopause. This is known as the *Walker circulation*. He also found that the monsoons are greatly affected by the distribution of air pressure and winds over the tropics and subtropics in both hemispheres.

This is where he made his most important discovery. In some years, for reasons scientists still do not understand, atmospheric pressure is lower than usual over Indonesia and that part of the Indian Ocean and higher than usual over Easter Island and the southeast Pacific. In other years the pattern is reversed, with higher than usual pressure over Indonesia and lower than usual pressure over Easter Island. This changing pattern of pressure distribution continues all the time, reaching its maxima at intervals of two to seven years. He called this periodic change the *Southern Oscillation* (it is always written with initial capital letters).

Low pressure over Indonesia brings heavy rain there, associated with rising air. On the opposite side of the Pacific, near the west coast of South America, air is subsiding. This pressure pattern strengthens the trade winds and these drive the Equatorial Current, which flows from east to west parallel to the equator. The sea surface is warm and often close to the highest temperature sea water can attain. This is about 85° F and it can rise no higher, because at this temperature water evaporates from the surface at such a fast rate that it cools the surface by drawing from it the latent heat of evaporation, holding down the temperature.

The Equatorial Current flows at the surface, carrying warm water away from South America and towards Indonesia. It is replaced by the Peru (or Humboldt) Current, which flows northwards close to the South America coast. This is a cool current. When it enters the tropics its waters are at about 68° F or lower, and sometimes as low as 61° F, making it the coldest seawater anywhere in the tropics. The Peruvian coast bulges into the Pacific and deflects the Peru Current to the west. Eventually it joins the Equatorial Current. As it starts to turn, the Peru Current draws up water from the near sea bed and, with it, nutrients scoured from the seabed sediments. The bottom water comes close to the surface as a series of upwellings, and its nutrients encourage vigorous growth of marine plants (phytoplankton). These, in turn, support a vast fish population, and the fish are food to huge flocks of seabirds.

Economically, the cold upwellings are extremely important. Peru has one of the world's largest fishing industries based mainly on the Pacific anchovy (*Engraulis ringens*), and the seabirds roost on shore, where accumulations of their droppings, called *guano*, are mined and sold as fertilizer. Not all the consequences are beneficial, however. Air joining the southeast trade winds flows above the Peru Current or across the Andes, producing very dry conditions along the coasts of Chile and Peru. Lima, Peru, receives an average of only 1.6 inches of rain a year, most of it in winter (May to September). Applying the equation for effective precipitation (see page 11), $r \div t = 0.2$, which makes the climate that of a very dry desert.

It is the surface of the ocean that is warmed by the Sun. Warm water forms a surface layer overlying much cooler water. Ordinarily, the Equatorial Current carries warm surface water away from South America and it accumulates around Indonesia. Consequently, the layer of warm water is deep around Indonesia and shallow near the South American west coast. It is the shallowness of the warm-water layer that allows the cold upwellings of nutrient-rich bottom water to rise almost to the surface.

During a Southern Oscillation, however, the pattern changes. Atmospheric pressure increases a little over Indonesia and decreases over Easter Island and the southeast Pacific. This reduction of the difference in pressure weakens the mechanism driving the trade winds. These slacken and occasionally cease entirely or even reverse their direction. The weakening of the trade winds reduces the force driving the Equatorial Current and it also weakens. Its weakening reduces the rate at which warm water is being shifted westward. The layer of warm water grows shallower around Indonesia and deeper near South America. From June to December 1972, for example, the sea surface off the Peruvian coast warmed to 6–7° F above its usual temperature. In effect, the warm surface water forms a small current of its own.

This current had been known locally for centuries. Usually it develops in the middle of summer, which in the southern hemisphere is Christmas time. That is why local people called it *El Niño* the boy-child. Like the infant Jesus, it brings good fortune, at least to some. Air crossing the ocean is no longer chilled and dried as it approaches the coast. Instead, moisture evaporates into it from the warm surface and falls as rain on the arid coastal strip. A place in northern Peru that received less than one inch of rain between November 1981 and June 1982 received 156 inches between November 1982 and June 1983. That is what El Niño can do. Despite causing floods and mudslides, on the whole it is good for farmers, but not everyone benefits.

When the depth of warm water increases, the cold upwellings of the Peru Current are suppressed. The nutrient-rich waters no longer reach the surface layer, and marine plants starve. As their population decreases, the fish feeding on them also starve, or migrate to richer waters far out at sea, and fish catches decrease sharply. As figure 11 shows, in 1970 Peruvian fishermen caught almost 14 million tons of fish. In 1973, following a strong El Niño, they caught only 2.4 million tons. To all intents and purposes the fishery collapsed, bring great hardship to the communities dependent on it. Catches recovered very slowly in the years that followed, as the table shows. It takes a long time for the numbers of fish to grow again and stocks remain vulnerable to El Niño episodes. They fell drastically in 1983, following the 1982 El Niño, although later ones have had little effect.

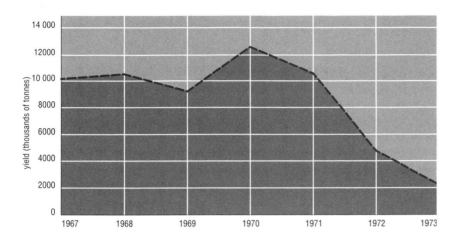

Figure 11: *Peruvian fish catches and the 1972 El Niño.*

Once the link between El Niño and the Southern Oscillation was realized, scientists joined their names. Today the phenomenon is known as an *El Niño–Southern Oscillation*, or ENSO. It is best known and most pronounced in the Pacific, but a much weaker ENSO is believed to occur in the tropical Atlantic, affecting the weather in West Africa.

Southern Oscillations can work in both directions, of course. Sometimes the ordinary distribution of pressure strengthens, the

Peruvian catches of sea fish
(millions of US tons)

Year	Catch	Year	Catch
1971	11.6	1983	1.6
1972	5.2	1984	3.3
1973	2.4	1985	4.6
1974	4.6	1986	6.1
1975	3.8	1987	5.0
1976	4.8	1988	7.3
1977	2.8	1989	7.5
1978	3.7	1990	7.5
1979	4.0	1991	7.7
1980	3.0	1992	7.5
1981	3.0	1993	9.2
1982	3.8		

Figure 12: *Reforestation project aimed at preventing desertification near Lima, Peru, 1984.* (UN photo 153871/Shaw McCutcheon)

trade winds blow harder, and the pool of warm water around Indonesia grows deeper while waters off South America grow cooler. For want of a better name, scientists have called this *La Niña*.

Serious though it is for the fishermen of Peru, the effects of ENSO extend much further than the eastern tropical Pacific and last much longer than the years in which they occur. The disturbance they produce in the oceanic circulation sends out what are known as *Rossby waves* after Carl-Gustav Rossby, the Swedish-American meteorologist who discovered such waves in the atmosphere. These waves move slowly, at about one-tenth of a mile per hour, and are very long, measuring some thousands of miles from one wave crest to the next. Ten years after the 1982–83 ENSO, these waves had crossed the Pacific and altered the path of the Kuroshio Current, raising the sea-surface temperature in the northwest Pacific by about 2° F. This was an increase comparable to the original warming in the tropics. It was believed to be affecting the climate of North America and scientists expected its effects to continue for at least another ten years.

It was the 1972 ENSO that brought drought to the Sahel region of Africa, along the southern margin of the Sahara, but that was not all it did. From May to September, rainfall was only half the average, and in many places less than one-quarter, over an area stretching from European Russia and into central Asia. Drought destroyed crops, reducing the Soviet grain harvest by 13%. The Chinese harvest was also poor and so was that in India, due to a weak monsoon. There was also drought in Australia that reduced the wheat harvest by 25%. Combined with the collapse in the Peruvian fishery, the world output of food in 1972 was almost 2% less than that in 1971.

Severe drought and a summer heat wave affected the United States in 1988 and continued into the following year in parts of California and in the north-central and southwestern states. At first, some scientists suspected this was an early indication of global warming (see page 121), but later it was found to be associated with the 1987 ENSO. The ENSO in the early 1990s contributed to extremely wet weather in the United States and widespread flooding in midwestern states from April to September 1993. Later, the same ENSO brought flooding to California in January and March 1995; a mild, dry winter to the eastern states; and a drought in Hawaii that lasted from October 1994 to March 1995.

Drought is always harmful, but unusually heavy rain can bring droughts to an end, and ENSO events can also deliver them. In Israel, winters with heavier than usual rainfall between 1975 and 1995 have been found to coincide with ENSO events. There is a *Southern Oscillation Index* or *El Niño Index*, which is calculated by subtracting the average monthly atmospheric pressure in Darwin, Australia, from that measured at Tahiti. Ordinarily, the result is positive (greater than 1), but during an ENSO it is strongly negative

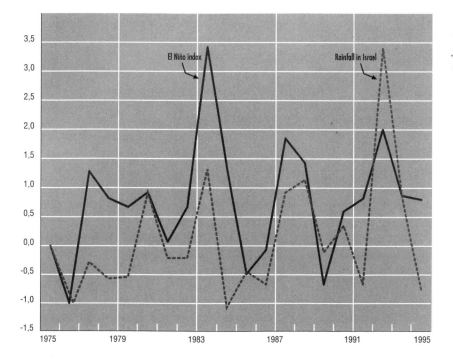

Figure 13: *El Niño and rainfall in Israel (deviations from average values, in relative units).*

(less than 1). Another index is based on changes in sea-surface temperature in the equatorial Pacific. These indexes can be used not only to identify ENSOs, but to compare one with another. Figure 13 shows the result of the comparison, made by a team of scientists led by Dr. Dan Yakir at the Weizmann Institute of Science in Israel, between the El Niño Index and the extent to which rainfall deviated from the annual average over the 20-year period. The graph shows how closely rainfall in Israel is linked to ENSO events. This was also reflected in the rate of growth of pine trees near Jerusalem. Israel suffered a long drought in the 1930s and weather records show no evidence of an ENSO during that decade.

In southern Africa, ENSO brings drought. That of the early 1990s caused the worst drought the region had suffered this century. Crop yields were halved and nearly 100 million people were affected. Another strong association has been found between ENSO events and corn (maize) yields in Zimbabwe. Corn is the most important food crop in Zimbabwe and yields depend on the amount of rainfall between January and March. Drought, with low crop yields, is usually unexpected, but if ENSO events could be predicted, farmers and governments could prepare for them. Surplus food from a previous good harvest could be taken into government stores, for example, or food could be imported before the drought caused world prices to rise. ENSO prediction has already benefited Brazil. There, the drought caused by the 1987 ENSO reduced crop yields by 85%, but by 1992 the ENSO was predicted long enough in advance for farmers to prepare, by instaling irrigation or changing to crop varieties that need less water, and the harvest was only slightly lower than normal.

In November 1995, scientists meeting at a conference in Washington, D.C., agreed to plans for establishing an international center to forecast ENSO events and supply the forecasts to everyone who may need them. Improved observations from the Topex-Poseidon satellite, launched in 1992, now allow scientists to detect quite small changes in ocean currents (see volume 6 for more details), and the ENSO indexes are constantly being improved. Already it is sometimes possible to predict an ENSO a year in advance. Soon scientists hope to be able to provide such forecasts regularly and reliably.

This would be an important achievement and one that may be even more important in years to come. The length and severity of the 1990s ENSO has led some scientists to suspect that if the world climate continues to grow warmer, ENSOs will become more frequent. It is important, therefore, to reduce to a minimum the disruption they have been causing for hundreds and probably thousands of years.

Jet streams and storm tracks

Where air is rising, the atmospheric pressure at the surface is reduced. Where air is subsiding, the surface pressure is increased. These vertical movements of air produce patterns of high and low pressure that move and change constantly. Over the world as a whole, however, the large-scale atmospheric circulation produces regions in which pressure is usually higher or lower than it is elsewhere.

At the equator, air rises into the Hadley cell (see page 8) system and surface pressure is low. That air subsides into the subtropics, producing high pressure. Subsiding air over the poles produces high pressure there and in midlatitudes, where the tropical and polar cells drive a third cell, air is generally rising and pressure is low. The overall pattern is illustrated in figure 14. This pressure distribution is only an average, of course, and pressure often varies locally.

The vertical movement of air and distribution of pressure also produce a pattern of prevailing winds. Again, these are averages, although the easterly trade winds are very reliable. Near ground level, the wind may be deflected by hills or tall buildings, but in

Figure 14: *Distribution of winds and pressure.*

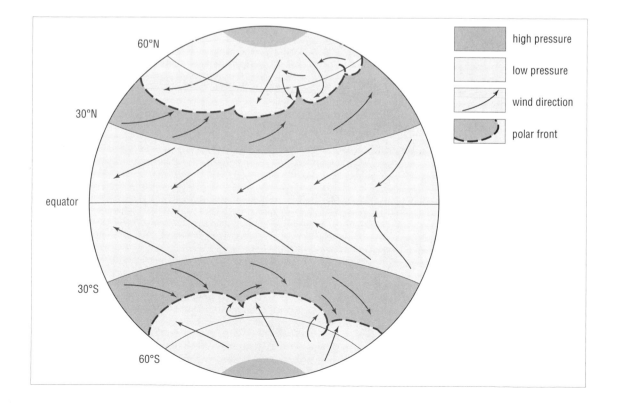

most places it will blow more frequently from one direction than from others. It means measuring the wind at regular intervals for a long time, but you can find out the commonest, or prevailing, wind direction around your home. Experiment 3 in *A Chronology of Weather* explains how to do it.

Over the world as a whole, the winds cancel one another. As many blow from the east as from the west and there is no need to measure the winds to prove the fact. When the wind blows over the ground, friction slows it, but friction works on both the objects that are in contact. By blowing against the ground, the wind pushes it, and over a large area the force is considerable. Think how the wind blowing against a mountain must be pressing against it. Continued for long enough, a wind from the west, in the same direction as the Earth's rotation, could make the Earth spin faster on its axis and a wind from the east could slow it. If the winds blew more from one direction than the other, the Earth would be accelerated or slowed. In fact, this did happen in January 1990. Winds blowing strongly across Asia and the Pacific slowed the Earth by an amount that made one day (a full rotation) one-two thousandth of a second longer. That is a tiny difference, but if it continued for thousands of years it would build into a substantial slowing. Other factors also slightly accelerate or slow the rotational speed of the Earth from time to time, but since there is no sustained change due to air movements, over the years easterlies and westerlies must balance. They must also be constantly replenished by pressure systems. Friction converts the energy of motion into heat, which is why rubbing your hands together warms them, and if more energy were not being fed into them all the time, friction would quickly slow the winds to a standstill.

Well clear of the ground, the wind is not subject to friction with the surface and so it usually blows with more force. Its direction also changes to become *geostrophic*; air moves away from areas of high atmospheric pressure and towards areas of low pressure. The force with which it does so depends on the difference in pressure between the two centers. You can think of the pressure difference as a sloping surface, or gradient. The steeper the gradient the faster the air flows, like a ball rolling downhill, and the force pushing it is called the *pressure gradient force*.

Once the air starts to move, however, it comes under the influence of the Coriolis effect (see the box on page 32). This deflects air moving away from the equator to the right in the northern hemisphere and left in the southern. The two forces act against one another and achieve a balance, with the air flowing parallel to the gradient rather than across it, at a speed proportional to the gradient (which appears on weather maps as the distance between isobars).

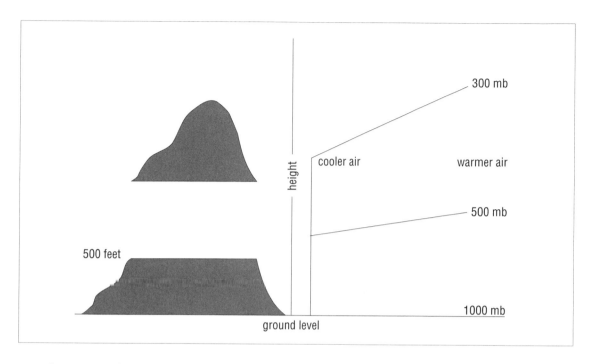

Figure 15: *Height contours and isobars.*

When you climb a hill, the gradient is often steeper in some places than in others. A line at right angles to the contours can also change direction. Atmospheric pressure often changes with height in the same way. That is why you sometimes see high-level clouds moving faster than clouds below them (the pressure gradient has steepened) or in a different direction.

Isobars, the lines on weather maps that join places where the atmospheric pressure is the same, are often likened to the height contours on ordinary maps, but this can be misleading. If you could remove all the land above a certain height contour, the result would be a level plane. Obviously, everywhere on the plane would be at the same height. If you could do the same with isobars, the resulting surface would be at the same pressure everywhere, but not at the same height. Figure 15 illustrates this. On the left a hill has been cut through at the 500-foot contour, exposing a flat surface, all at the same height. On the right, three surfaces are exposed. Each is at a different pressure (1000 mb, 500 mb, 300 mb) and on a weather map the pressure distribution would be shown by contour-like isobars. These are pressure surfaces, however, where the pressure is the same everywhere, and measured in relation to other pressures, not to distance from the ground surface. As you see, in this case the surfaces slope in relation to ground level.

The layers of air between the 1000-mb level and 500-mb level and between the 500-mb level and 300-mb level are thicker on the right of the diagram than they are on the left. This shows that the layers of air at a particular pressure are not all of the same thickness.

What is more, the layer between 500 mb and 300 mb thickens to the right more than does the layer below it, so its pressure surface slopes more steeply.

Air expands when it warms, so the thickness of a layer of air between two pressure surfaces is proportional to its temperature. In figure 15, the air to the right is warmer than the air to the left. Now imagine a horizontal line drawn across one of these layers from left to right and you will see that pressure changes along it. Starting, say, at the 400-mb level on the left, a line parallel to the ground surface would be almost at 500 mb on the right. This pressure difference produces a wind and, because of the relationship between temperature and the thickness of the layers, it is called the *thermal wind.* A thermal wind will blow where two bodies of air are at different temperatures at the same height, and its force is proportional to the temperature difference between them. In the northern hemisphere a thermal wind will blow with the cooler air on its left, in the southern hemisphere with the cooler air on its right.

There are belts around the Earth where the general circulation of the atmosphere produces very sharp temperature differences of this kind. Where the air in the Hadley cells starts to subside, it is adjacent to subsiding air flowing towards the equator. That is one region where a sharp temperature difference causes a strong thermal wind. The other is where cold air flowing away from the poles meets warm air flowing away from the tropics. The low-latitude boundary between air at quite different temperatures is called the *intertropical front*, and that in high latitudes is the *polar front.* These are the two regions where the thermal wind is strongest and it is especially strong near the tropopause, at a height of about 30,000 feet, where the temperature difference is most marked.

At the polar front, the height of the tropopause (the upper boundary of the lower atmosphere) is higher on the side where the air is warmer than it is on the cooler side, because the warm air forms a thicker layer. Warm air slightly overlaps cold air and the thermal wind is strongest of all where it wraps around. Like a long tube of moving air snaking around the world, this wind blows from west to east in both hemispheres at speeds up to 150 MPH. In winter, when the temperature difference is greatest, it can reach 300 MPH. This is the *polar front jet stream.* The subtropical jet stream blows more constantly, but not so fast.

Its position is quite variable, but in summer the polar front jet stream usually lies across North America, very nearly following the Canadian border. In winter it is farther to the south, approximately along a line from the tip of Baja California then running northeast to Cape Hatteras. It crosses Europe and Asia in summer along a line through the Mediterranean and Caspian Seas, north of the Himalayas to Japan, and in winter passes across North Africa, northern Arabia, and just to the south of the Himalayas to Indonesia.

If you were a jet pilot, often flying at high altitudes, the location and strength of the jet stream would be important to you. It is more difficult to see why those of us who stay on the ground should worry about a wind, even a strong one, several miles above our heads. In fact, though, the jet stream has a powerful effect on the weather. Weather fronts and depressions tend to form beneath it and move along it. These often bring rain and they can bring storms, sometimes severe ones. The tracks most frequently followed by storms in the United States are more or less parallel to the jet stream above them.

Jet streams are not constant, however. They twist and snake, but according to well-defined rules, and every so often they die away altogether. When they do that, weather systems become stuck in one place. We may experience a spell of wet weather or a spell of fine weather. We may also experience a drought.

Blocking highs

In mid-latitudes, the prevailing winds blow from west to east in both hemispheres, carrying weather systems with them. This is called *zonal flow*. It is what brings us our "ordinary" weather, but from time to time the pattern breaks down. Instead of moving mainly from west to east, the air moves north and south, in what is called a *meridional flow*. This brings unusual weather from a higher or lower latitude. It can also happen that the movement of air ceases entirely over a large region. The weather becomes "stuck" and remains the same for weeks or months on end. If that weather happens to be fine and dry, prolonging it causes drought.

Northwest Europe, from western France north to Sweden, experienced a drought of this kind in 1975 and 1976. For day after day in June and July 1976, temperatures over England reached more than 90° F, and television weather reports showed satellite photographs of the whole of Britain with not a single cloud anywhere. The weather became stuck in the same way in Finland in July 1972, when people living close to the Arctic Circle enjoyed temperatures of 90° F. It is also partly what caused the 1972 drought in the Sahel region of Africa. That was associated with an ENSO event (see page 36), but it involved the same kind of "seizure" of the weather. The droughts on the American plains east of the Rockies that produced the Dust Bowl conditions of the 1930s (see page 76) and that also occurred in the 1890s, 1910s, 1950s, and 1990s were also caused by this kind of blocking.

The polar front, with the polar front jet stream at its top, separates Arctic and subtropical air. In the northern hemisphere, weather to the north of the front is colder than weather to the south of it. When the zonal flow is drawn on a map, however, it is not quite straight. Midlatitude air does move in an easterly direction around the world, but it is deflected by mountain ranges that produce waves in the pattern, so the air follows a slightly wavy path.

These waves were discovered by Carl-Gustav Rossby in 1940 (see volume 6 for more details) and are known as Rossby waves. They are very long, with about 4,000 miles between one wave crest and the next, and they affect the whole of the polar front. The waves are produced by surface features, which deflect the stream of air. But, provided the flow of air then continues to follow the same track in relation to the surface, the wave pattern is quite stable. Near the surface, large eddies up to 1,200 miles across produce areas of relatively high and low atmospheric pressure along the polar front, all traveling eastward and carrying with them the weather we expect for the time of year.

When the polar front moves away from the equator in spring, however, the waves become unstable. The Coriolis effect (see box on page 32) increases in strength as the air flow moves into a higher latitude, so air is deflected. Because it is already following a curved path, the air possesses vorticity (see box). Increasing the magnitude of the Coriolis effect is equivalent to increasing the planetary

Vorticity and angular momentum

Any fluid moving in relation to the Earth's surface tends to rotate about a vertical axis. This is called *vorticity*. Vorticity in a counter-clockwise direction (seen from above) is said to be positive and clockwise vorticity is said to be negative.

On a large scale, the rotation of the Earth also imparts vorticity to a moving fluid everywhere except at the equator. This vorticity is equal in magnitude to the Coriolis effect and is positive in the northern hemisphere and negative in the southern. It is called *planetary vorticity* and the vorticity of the fluid itself is called *relative vorticity*. The two together are called *absolute vorticity*. For any body of air or liquid possessing vorticity, absolute vorticity tends to remain constant. In other words, if one of its components increases, the other decreases in proportion.

The speed with which a body rotates around an axis is called its *angular velocity* and is measured in the number of degrees through which it travels in a given length of time. The Earth, for example, rotates through 360° in 24 hours. This is its angular velocity. The body also has *angular momentum*. This is calculated by multiplying together its angular velocity, its mass, and its radius of rotation measured from the axis of its rotation to its most distant point. For a body of a particular mass, angular velocity, and radius of rotation, the angular momentum is a constant. That is, $M \times V \times R =$ a constant, where M is mass, V is angular velocity, and R is the radius. Ignoring friction, which slows all motion, this constant remains the same; technically, angular momentum is said to be conserved. This means that if one variable alters, the others must alter to compensate so the constant remains the same. If the radius decreases, for example, and the mass remains unaltered, the angular velocity will increase.

vorticity, and to maintain a constant absolute vorticity, the relative vorticity of the airflow decreases. This turns the moving air back toward the equator, which reduces its planetary vorticity and increases its relative vorticity, turning it away from the equator again.

Over a period of about three to eight weeks, the undulations of the Rossby waves grow bigger until much of the flow is meridional rather than zonal. Figure 16 illustrates this. In A, the waves are small and the general flow is zonal. Flow becomes increasingly meridional in B, as the waves grow bigger, and in C flow is mainly meridional. Then, in D, the waves break into cells, where the air flows in a series of circles with the larger waves weaving around them. At this stage the zonal flow has broken down completely and the cells cease to move. They are stuck and can remain so for some time.

Weather systems continue to travel eastward, but the cells remain stationary and advancing systems go around them. This is called *blocking* and once it is firmly established it can remain in position for a long time. The polar front jet stream has then split into two, very wavy branches with the stationary cells between them. As the diagram shows, cells of warm air are trapped in the north and cool air in the south, with the main flow of air, including the jet stream, traveling around them. The circulation is clockwise (anticyclonic) around the warm cells and counterclockwise (cyclonic) around the cold cells. This produces stationary anticyclones in the north.

Figure 16: *Rossby waves and blocking.*

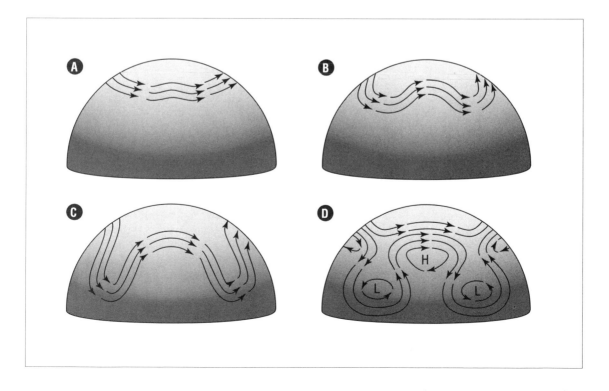

Weather systems moving from west to east are diverted around them. This is called *blocking* and the cells causing it are called *blocking anticyclones* or *blocking highs.*

As the undulations become more pronounced, Arctic air is carried a long way south and tropical air a long way north because the jet stream also marks the position of the polar front, with cold air on one side and warm air on the other. Some regions experience temperatures much lower than are usual and others temperatures that are higher, and rainfall also changes. High pressure, with subsiding air, brings fine, dry weather that, is very warm in summer and very cold in winter. Drought is less likely in winter, because the rate of evaporation is relatively low, but blocking in winter does bring dry weather. If this is followed by further prolonged blocking in summer, drought is probably inevitable. In the south, *blocking cyclones* or *blocking lows* bring prolonged periods of wet weather.

The location of a blocking anticyclone is very important. In 1975 and 1976, one centered over northwest Europe brought the most severe drought since the first reliable records were made, in 1727, and reduced the water content of soil in Britain to its lowest value since 1698 (as measured at the Royal Botanic Gardens, Kew, London, which was established in the late 17th century). This blocking diverted depressions approaching from the Atlantic 5° to 10° to the north. Further east, however, the summer was cool. Winds over Russia were mainly from the north and temperatures were up to 7° F below normal. In 1954, on the other hand, a blocking anticyclone over Scandinavia and eastern Europe gave Britain a cool, wet summer.

Mountains running north and south, approximately at right angles to the west-to-east flow of air, can also cause blocking anticyclones to form. It is blocking to the east of the Rocky Mountains that from time to time brings severe drought to the Great Plains. As air crosses the mountains, it rises and is compressed into an ever-thinner layer. To some extent the whole atmosphere rises a little, but not enough to compensate, and air spills horizontally from the rising mass. When air flows outward from a region of high pressure, planetary vorticity makes it turn clockwise, so the airflow swings southward. On the other side of the mountains, the air descends, expanding as it does so. Pressure decreases and air is drawn inward. When air flows inward toward a region of low pressure, planetary vorticity makes it turn counterclockwise, to the north. This can set up a series of long waves, like those in the polar jet stream that can trap blocking anticyclones in the southeast. These divert northward the depressions that ordinarily bring rain. The Sahel drought (see page 81) was partly caused by the blocking of Atlantic depressions by a northward movement of the subtropical anticyclone over the Sahara.

Blocking weather seems to occur for several years in succession, then disappears for several more years. It is rather like the periodic changes of the Southern Oscillation (see page 37) that lead to ENSO events, but in both cases the oscillation is irregular. It is simple enough to identify blocking patterns when they occur and even to forecast them a short time ahead, but not to predict them reliably years in advance. Nevertheless, droughts in the Great Plains do seem to recur at intervals of 20 to 23 years. So do variations in the temperature records for central England, which are complete back to 1659, and in temperatures in other parts of the world. Over Europe, blocking seems to be more common in the 30s and 80s of each century than at other times, and severe winters are more likely in the 40s and 60s. One day, scientists may succeed in unraveling the complexities of these cycles. If and when they do, they will be able to warn of blocking that brings drought in time for farmers and water utilities to make adequate preparation.

WATER AND LIFE

Why plants need water

Leave a plant without water and after a time it will wilt. Its leaves will hang limp and unless it is a woody plant, with a rigid stem to support it, the entire plant will collapse. All plants must have water, and the amount they need can be surprisingly large. A birch tree, for example, with about 250,000 leaves, moves approximately 630 pints of water from the soil to the atmosphere every day, and while they are growing peas use nearly 40 pints of water for every ounce of weight they gain. Living cells are 80% water by weight and 60% of the weight of a human body is water. Even the most important or frightening person you can think of is 60% water!

Plants obtain their water from the soil. It enters through their roots, moves through their stems and leaves, and evaporates from two types of small pores, called *stomata* (the singular is *stoma*) and *lenticels*, in the leaves. The loss of water through these pores is called *transpiration*, but in practice it is impossible to measure transpiration separately from other kinds of evaporation and so the two are measured together, as *evapotranspiration*.

Area for area, water evaporates from small pores much faster than from an open water surface, such as a lake. This is because water molecules at the edges of the pore or lake spread to the sides and evaporate from there, but the smaller the diameter of the surface, the longer are its edges in proportion to its area, so water is able to spread more.

Evaporation is the movement of water molecules from a body of liquid water into the air, as water vapor. Vapor molecules in the layer of air immediately above the surface of the liquid exert a pressure on the surface. This *vapor pressure* increases as the number of molecules exerting it increases until it reaches the *saturation vapor pressure*. At this point the relative humidity (RH) reaches 100% and the water vapor is saturated, although the situation is usually described as the air being saturated. Until this point, more water molecules are entering the air than are returning to the surface of the liquid, but when the saturation vapor pressure is reached the number leaving the liquid and the number returning to it are the same and no more evaporation occurs.

The rate of transpiration from the surface of a plant depends on the difference between the water vapor pressure inside the plant tissues and in the air outside. This depends partly on the temperature because the pressure exerted by the same amount of water vapor is inversely proportional to the temperature. In other words, relative humidity (RH) decreases as temperature increases.

Inside a plant leaf, air spaces ordinarily contain water vapor at the saturation vapor pressure and a relative humidity of 100%. If, say, the temperature inside and outside the leaf is 50° F and the relative humidity in the outside air is 60%, the vapor pressure inside the leaf (RH = 100%) will be 12.3 millibars (mb) and that outside will be 7.4 mb, so there is a pressure difference of (12.3 − 7.4 =) 4.9 mb. With the same amount of moisture in the outside air, if the temperature increases to 80° F, the vapor pressure inside the leaf will be 35.7 mb (RH is still 100%), that outside still only 7.4 mb (RH is then 21%), so the pressure difference increases to 28.3 mb. Even if the air becomes more moist as it warms, and its RH remains at 60%, the difference in vapor pressure will still increase. At 80° F vapor pressure inside the leaf will be 35.7 mb, that outside 21.4 mb, and the difference will be 14.3 mb.

Leaves are exposed to the sunlight, which they need for photosynthesis. Their absorption of light also warms them, and the more intense the light the more they are warmed by it. Dark leaves absorb more light than pale leaves and if a dark leaf is exposed to direct, intense sunlight for several hours, the temperature below its surface can be much higher than that of the outside air. The water vapor inside the leaf is still at saturation vapor pressure, but as the temperature increases so does the vapor pressure and, therefore, so does the difference between the internal and external vapor pressure. Strong sunlight alone can increase the rate at which a plant loses moisture.

It is this difference in vapor pressure that controls the rate at which water evaporates. The warmer and drier the outside air, the faster the plant will lose water through its open pores. If the RH of the air increases, the plant will lose water more slowly, but during a drought the RH of the air falls very low. Even in temperate climates, and with ample water in the soil, plants often wilt in the middle of a summer day, when the rate of transpiration exceeds the rate at which their roots can absorb moisture. (This type of wilting cannot be cured by watering the plant, because shortage of water is not what causes it.)

Plants use water for mechanical and chemical purposes. Mechanically, it is what supports the structure of their leaves and other soft tissues. In large plants, such as trees, the hydrogen bonds linking liquid water molecules into groups are strong enough to allow columns of water to be drawn from the roots all the way to the crown. It is transpiration that drives the upward flow. As water evaporates from the leaves, more water is drawn up to replace it.

When plant cells have all the water they need, they are filled and press against their walls. This makes them rigid (the technical term is *turgid*). If they lose water, cell walls become flabby and the whole structure loses rigidity. The plant wilts and, unless it replaces the lost water, eventually it will die.

Chemically, plants, like all living organisms, use water to transport the chemical compounds they need. Water is an excellent solvent and all the liquids found in plants and animals are solutions of various compounds in water.

Some plants have evolved to tolerate dry conditions. These are called *xerophytes* (the Greek *xeros* means dry and *phuton* means plant) and they grow in deserts (see page 14). Many have stomata only on the undersides of their leaves, where they are shaded and cooler, or in pits or grooves where they are sheltered from the drying wind. Some shed their leaves in very dry weather or reduce their leaves to a very small size. The leaves of cacti are their spines, for example, and they use their green stems for photosynthesis.

Plants that grow in moister climates do not possess most of these adaptations, but they do have some. Many evergreens, for example, have dark green, thick, waxy leaves. The dark color increases their absorption of light, to help photosynthesis; their thickness increases the amount of water they can hold, and their waxy outer coating reduces the rate at which water evaporates from them. Coniferous trees have leaves reduced to tiny scales or needles to reduce transpiration, and broad-leaved trees shed their leaves in winter, shutting down both photosynthesis and transpiration. Broad-leaved evergreens, such as holly (*Ilex*), grow best in a warm, moist climate. Deciduous trees (which shed their leaves in winter) and conifers grow in cooler climates, where water often freezes in winter. Plants can absorb water only as a liquid, so a winter when water is frozen is equivalent to a dry season when no rain falls.

A predictable dry season, or cold winter, presents no problem for plants. They have been able to adapt to these simply because they are predictable. It is when bad times arrive unexpectedly that plants (and animals) suffer, and droughts are always unexpected. They are periods of dry weather at a time of year when there is usually rain.

As the ground dries by evaporation, water is lost rather than the chemical compounds dissolved in the water. Evaporation from the surface draws water from below, through the tiny spaces between soil particles (see page 56). When it evaporates, the dissolved compounds are left behind and accumulate in such water as remains. This increase in concentration makes it more difficult for plant roots to absorb liquid, and plants begin to suffer.

Less water enters plants, but their rate of transpiration does not slow at once. Plants can open and close their stomata, but they do so according to their own internal clock, which opens them during the day and closes them at night. Even plants kept in total darkness or permanent light continue to open and close their stomata according to this rhythm, and plants that grow best in moist climates have many stomata. The average for many plants is nearly 200,000 for every square inch of leaf area. Some have more. Spanish oak, a hybrid of Turkey oak (*Quercus cerris*) and cork oak (*Q. suber*) which grows in southern Europe, has about 775,000 per square inch.

When a plant is losing more water by transpiration than it is absorbing through its roots it is said to experience "water stress." If this happens suddenly, the cells around the stomata may lose their rigidity and instead of the stomata closing, they open wide. If water stress develops more slowly, the stomata will close, but they cannot be kept closed indefinitely without harming the plant. These are the pores through which water evaporates, but they are also the pores through which the plant absorbs the carbon dioxide it needs for photosynthesis and excretes oxygen, the byproduct of photosynthesis. A plant may survive the onset of a drought by sealing itself, but it cannot grow in this condition and, if the drought continues, eventually the plant will starve.

Crop plants need large amounts of water. About 1.5 tons of water are required to grow 1 ton of wheat and about 10,000 tons to grow a ton of cotton fiber. Even in climates where rainfall seems abundant, many crops benefit from additional watering, because there are months during which the amount of water that can evaporate from the surface is greater than the amount of rainfall.

Even if the weather is only slightly drier than usual, plant growth can be slowed and crop yields reduced. In severe drought plants adapted to moist climates cannot survive. Except in regions where people can afford to import the food they need, drought is soon followed by famine.

Water below ground

Morgan Twp. H.S. Library
Valparaiso, IN 46383

Washington, D.C., receives an average 42 inches of precipitation a year, distributed fairly evenly with no month wetter or drier than any other. In April, for example, there is on average 3.3 inches of rain. This is enough rain to cover the ground to a depth of 3.3 inches in one month and over the year Washington receives enough rain to cover it to a depth of 42 inches. When figures for precipitation are given as so many inches, that is what the "inches" mean. It is the depth to which that much precipitation would cover the surface. Except when unusually heavy rain causes rivers to burst their banks and flood the surrounding land, however, rain and melting snow do not lie on the surface. They disappear as quickly as they arrive.

Most of our rain and snow comprise water that evaporated from the sea and a smaller amount is water that evaporated from wet ground and lakes, and that is transpired by plants (see page 51). After it has fallen, rivers carry the water back to the sea. Obviously, rivers cannot return to the sea more water than fell as rain and snow, but if they returned less than this, most places that in fact are dry land would lie permanently beneath water.

This much is obvious, but if you look at a river it is not at all obvious how it gathers the water it carries. You cannot usually see water flowing into it, even during heavy rain. Nor is it obvious how plants obtain the water they need. During dry weather the soil often feels very dry. Crumble it between your fingers and it turns to dust. Despite this, plants continue to grow, which means they are able to find water somewhere.

When rain falls and snow melts, there are three ways for the water to disappear from sight. Some evaporates, returning immediately to the air as vapor. In very hot, dry weather evaporation removes a large amount of water. Some water flows over the surface, moving downhill. Water is most likely to flow in this way after very heavy rain. Heavy rain consists of large drops that fall fast enough to batter the soil surface. Battering breaks down small, crumbsized lumps of soil into their individual grains, then packs them tightly together, leaving almost no spaces between particles. Once this has happened, water cannot penetrate the soil surface, so it flows across it. As it flows, the water carries away soil particles, which can lead to serious erosion (see page 72).

Soil consists of particles of varying sizes. Sandy soil is made up of the largest grains, silt of much finer grains, and clay of the smallest grains of all. Sand grains are from 0.002 to 0.08 inch in diameter, silt particles 0.001 to 0.002 inch, and clay particles are less than 0.001 inch across. The smaller the particles, the more tightly they can pack together and so the more risk there is that heavy rain will produce an impermeable layer on the soil surface. This is very unlikely with sandy soils, more likely with silt soils, and a common occurrence with clay soils.

Most of the water disappears downward. It drains vertically through the soil. This is the source of the water below ground on which plants depend and also the source of most of the water that flows into rivers and from there to the sea.

There are small spaces between soil particles through which water can drain. The smaller the particles the smaller the spaces between them, and the more slowly water moves downward. Spill water onto a sandy beach and it vanishes almost at once because the spaces between sand grains are large. Spill water onto a clay soil and it soaks into the ground much more slowly. Because water spends more time near the surface of a clay soil than a sandy soil, this also means more of it evaporates.

The water moves downward through the soil until it reaches a layer of impermeable material. This may be hard, compacted clay, but usually it is rock. The water can sink no further, so it starts to accumulate. In the layer closest to the impermeable layer all the spaces between soil particles fill with water. This soil is then saturated. It can hold no more water, so the layer above it becomes saturated in its turn. Above the impermeable layer there is a layer of soil that is fully saturated with water. This is the *groundwater.*

The groundwater has an upper surface. This is the boundary between saturated soil below and unsaturated soil above, and it is known as the *water table*. The boundary is not a sharp one, like the boundary between the surface of a lake and the air above it, because water is constantly being drawn upward from the saturated zone into the lower part of the unsaturated zone in the *capillary fringe*. Figure 17 shows how water is distributed in the layers of soil beneath the surface.

Water in the capillary fringe is flowing upward, against the pull of gravity. The mechanism is the same as when you soak up spilled water by dipping a piece of blotting paper into it. The phenomenon is called *capillarity* and this ability to flow uphill is one more of the remarkable properties of water.

Water molecules are polar, with a positive electric charge at one end and a negative charge at the other, and in the liquid state hydrogen bonds link them together as groups. Each molecule is attracted to those around it and, except at the surface, these attractions cancel one another, so a molecule is pulled with equal force in all directions. At the surface, however, there is no pull upward and all the attractive force is to the sides and downward.

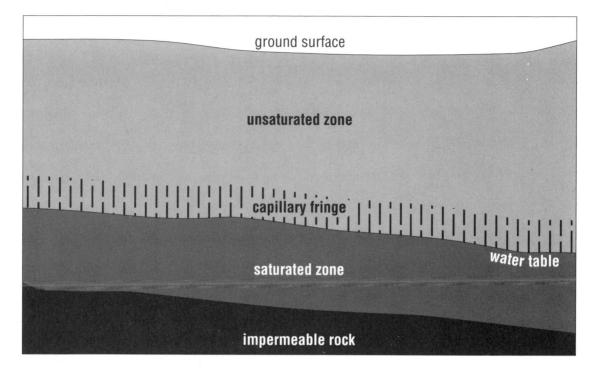

ground surface

unsaturated zone

capillary fringe

saturated zone

water table

impermeable rock

This holds the molecules at the surface very firmly. It is called surface tension and is surprisingly strong. Many small insects can walk on the surface of water because the surface tension is sufficient to support their weight, and experiment 26 in *A Chronology of Weather* explains how it will also allow a metal paper clip to float.

Surface tension pulls the surface molecules into the shape that requires the least amount of energy to sustain. This is the shape with the smallest surface area in relation to volume, which is a sphere. A drop of water on a greasy (water-repellent) surface will adopt a spherical shape, flattened somewhat by its own weight.

This is also the force that drives water upward through very narrow tubes or pathways. Polar molecules are attracted to opposite electric charges in the walls of the tube. This draws them a short distance up the sides of the tube and they pull behind them the molecules to which they are linked by hydrogen bonds. The water surface is now concave (sags in the center), as is shown in figure 18. Surface tension pushes the center of the water surface upward, to restore the convex (bulges in the center) shape closest to a sphere. This raises the level of the water at the center, exposing molecules to the side of the center to the attraction of charged molecules in the side of the tube. The water flows a little further up the sides, surface tension seeks to restore the surface shape, and the water rises still further. A limit is reached when the weight of the column of water is equal to the force pushing the water upward.

Figure 17: *Soil, groundwater, and the water table.*

Capillarity occurs only in very narrow tubes, because a wide tube holds so much water that its weight exceeds the upward force as soon as it rises at all. If you wish to test it for yourself, try to find a glass tube, open at both ends, with a bore no larger than 0.03 inch. Hold this vertically and insert one end into a bowl of cold water (surface tension decreases as temperature rises). The water is easier to see if you color it. Water should rise about 3.5 inches up the tube; it will rise further if the tube is narrower and not so far if it is wider.

The spaces between soil particles link to form long, irregular channels narrow enough for capillarity to occur, but the channels do not rise vertically. They twist and turn this way and that. Sometimes they are vertical, sometimes horizontal, and most of the time at varying angles between these two extremes. Weight always acts vertically, of course, so as water rises through the channels by capillarity, much of its weight is supported by the soil particles themselves. This allows the water to move much further than it would in a straight tube held vertically.

Suppose the soil is completely soaked after heavy rain or the melting of snow. All the capillary channels will be filled with water. Water evaporates from the surface at almost the same rate as from an open water surface, such as a lake. This reduces the weight in the water column, allowing more water to be drawn from below by capillarity to replace it.

Capillary matting, which you can buy to water plants automatically, is based on this principle. One end of the matting lies in a

Figure 18:   *Capillarity.*

reservoir of water and the rest of it beneath the soil or pots in which plants are growing. This soil is saturated with water and as water leaves by evapotranspiration more water flows from the reservoir and through the capillary channels in the matting and then the soil to replace it. The matting is designed so that water will flow through it faster than it can be lost into the air from the soil and plant surfaces. As long as the reservoir contains water, the plants have as much water as they need.

Outdoors, where there is no capillary matting to help, the rate of evaporation at the wet surface eventually exceeds the rate at which capillary moisture can keep the soil saturated and the surface dries. Once a layer of dry soil covers the surface, evaporation almost ceases. You need not dig far below the dry surface to find moist soil. The depth at which you will find it depends partly on the number and species of plants growing in it. Plants are constantly moving water from the soil to the air, so they dry the soil. Soil with no plants is much more moist than soil with plants.

Plants obtain their water from below, tapping the stream rising by capillarity from the water table. This allows them to flourish even when the uppermost layer of soil is dry as dust, but their health and eventually their survival depend on the height of the water table, which depends in turn on the amount of ground water. During prolonged drought the ground water is not replenished. Gradually the water table falls and, with it, the capillary fringe, and the capillary channels empty. As the water level in the soil falls, plants with shallow roots are the first to suffer, but if the drought is severe it will injure even plants with huge and deep root systems.

Wells and springs

Layers of rock are seldom horizontal. Where rock is exposed at the surface you can see for yourself that it almost always slopes, even if only slightly. Pour water onto it and the water will flow downhill. This is also true of rock layers below ground. They slope and so water that accumulates above a layer of impermeable rock will flow downhill. That is how water that falls as rain or snow over land eventually reaches the rivers that carry it to the sea. Ground water flows very slowly because it moves through a fairly dense mass of sand, gravel, or soil particles. Speeds vary from as little as one foot in a century to as fast as one mile per hour. Once a molecule of water enters the ground water it may be several centuries before it returns to the surface. For comparison, a water molecule entering the ocean may remain there for several thousands of years.

Above the impermeable layer, ground water moves through saturated soil. In most cases the water table marks the upper limit of saturation. Obviously, the position of the water table is determined by that of the underlying layer, which prevents water sinking deeper. It has nothing to do with the level of the ground surface. If the soil is shallow, heavy rains may cause the water table to rise all the way to the surface, making the soil waterlogged, but if the soil were deeper the water table could rise by the same amount without causing waterlogging.

Movements of the rocks forming the uppermost layers of the Earth's crust alter the position and slope of impermeable layers and erosion by wind and water alters the shape of the surface. Over millions of years, jagged mountains are eroded into smooth hills and eventually the hills are washed and blown away until the landscape is almost level. All the time this is happening, and the process is continuous, water falling on the surface is draining downward into the ground water and toward the sea.

Suppose these processes, of Earth movement and erosion, cut through the entire system. Perhaps faulting breaks the impermeable layer, leaving one side of the fracture at a lower level than the other, and erosion carries away softer material to leave a hillside. Water continues to move down the slope of the impermeable layer, but this now emerges at or close to the surface. Where this happens, ground water will reach the surface. It may seep into the overlying soil in a small, waterlogged area or, with thinner soil or a faster flow, it may trickle or bubble from the ground. In either case it emerges as a spring.

If a number of springs discharge into a natural hollow in the ground the water may form a pool or lake. In deserts, this is how oases form, providing evidence that even in the driest parts of the world there is often water below ground (see page 13). Higher up a slope, springs are commonly the source of small streams that eventually grow into large rivers.

Springs are often rather mysterious. People have always had a great respect for them, because they have no obvious cause and the water they deliver is either pure enough to drink or contains dissolved mineral salts believed to be beneficial to health. It is as though the ground itself were spontaneously providing a reliable source of wholesome water. In a sense, of course, this is precisely what is happening, but it is mysterious only because the reasons for it are hidden below ground and the water has usually traveled a considerable distance before it reaches the spring. As the diagram A in figure 19 suggests, the spring occurs at an accidental interruption in the long, slow journey of the ground water.

Water, which never occurs naturally as pure H_2O, changes chemically as it moves through the ground. First it travels downward, through the soil, reacting with some of the chemical compounds it

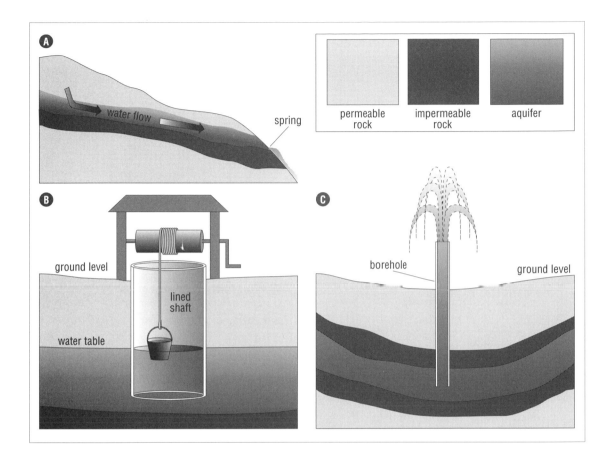

Figure 19: *A) Spring, B) Well, C) Artesian (overflowing) well.*

meets and dissolving others. As its journey continues, most of these substances are removed by further chemical reactions. If the water flows over hard rock, such as granite, and through soil particles derived from it, the emerging spring water will be fairly pure and "soft." If it flows over or through material containing large amounts of carbonates, such as calcium carbonate and magnesium carbonate, some of these will react with acids naturally present in the water and the spring water will be "hard."

Drink from a spring, especially in summer, and you are almost certain to be struck by how cold the water is. In fact, it is warmer than the average annual air temperature in the area around the spring. Groundwater flows so slowly that it is warmed by the heat of the rocks below ground. Most water taken from very deep wells must be cooled before it can be used.

Just above an impermeable layer groundwater flows through material called an *aquifer*; provided it is not too deep to be reached, fresh water can be obtained from it. The simplest way to extract water from an aquifer is to dig a well. This is also the most ancient method. As diagram B in figure 19 shows, the task involves nothing more than digging a hole. This determines the size of a well, because it must be wide enough for the person who does the digging. Some dug wells are only three feet in diameter, but most are at least 4 to 8 feet wide and some are very much wider. The hole must be lined, partly to prevent the sides falling in and filling it and partly to prevent contamination of the water, and it must be deep enough to penetrate below the water table. At the bottom, the sides may be perforated to allow water to enter, but just leaving them open at the bottom is usually enough. Water will fill the bottom of the well up to the level of the water table and a bucket, lowered on a rope from a winch at the top is used to collect it.

Wells vary in depth. Most are less than 100 feet deep, but some have been dug to as much as 500 feet. Although the technology is simple, digging a well is very hard work, and it becomes even more arduous, and possibly dangerous, once it penetrates below the water table.

It is not necessary to dig such a wide hole, because water can be pumped from the ground through a much narrower borehole. This is cut with drilling machinery and may be only 4 inches in diameter, or even less. The pump works by evacuating air from the upper part of the tube. Air pressure in the tube is then lower than the pressure on the water at the bottom of the borehole, and water is pushed up the tube. Unfortunately, water can be raised no more than about 26 feet in this way, so the technique has a serious disadvantage. If the water table is lower than that, an alternative method must be used. A much wider borehole can accommodate a pump submerged in the water at the bottom, which can lift water much higher, or the borehole can contain a smaller internal pipe through which air is pumped from the surface under pressure. The compressed air at the bottom of the well then pushes water up the main borehole. Using methods of this kind, wells can be sunk to much greater depth. In Australia there are wells up to 6,000 feet deep (and water from them is so hot it boils when it reaches the surface, where the air pressure is much lower than it is at depth).

It may not be necessary to use pumps or even buckets. The water may rise to the surface of its own accord. A well of this kind is called *artesian* or an *overflowing well*, shown in diagram C of figure 19.

An aquifer bounded only by impermeable material below is said to be *unconfined*. Water drains into it freely from above and the water table, marking its upper limit, can change in height according to the amount of water the aquifer contains. There are also *confined* aquifers. These comprise permeable material, through which groundwater flows, that is bounded by two impermeable layers, one above as well as the one below. Water in a confined aquifer is trapped.

Imagine what happens where the base of an aquifer is curved to form a deep hollow. If the aquifer is unconfined, groundwater will

Figure 20: *A well dug on a dried-up riverbed in Secota, Ethiopia, 1986.*   (UN photo 156652/John Isaac)

accumulate in the hollow until the water table is at the same level above the hollow as it is to either side. If the ground surface also curves down, following the shape of the underlying rock, the water table may lie higher than ground level. In that case the hollow will fill with water, forming a lake. This cannot happen to water in a confined aquifer. The water flows into the hollow from one side, but between two impermeable layers. Its level cannot rise, so the weight of inflowing water increases the pressure under which the water is held. This pressure pushes water up the other side of the dip in the aquifer, allowing it to continue its journey, but the pressure at the center of the dip can be considerable.

Drill a borehole through the upper impermeable layer and water will rise up the pipe. How high it rises depends on the shape of the hollow, but sometimes the top of the borehole, at ground level, will be lower than the confined aquifer outside the hollow. The inflowing water will then try to behave as though it its aquifer were unconfined. It would rise through the hole in the confining layer and saturate the overlying soil except that the borehole has an impermeable lining. This forces it to rise through the borehole and to flow freely from the surface. The well overflows.

An artesian well (the name is from Artois, an ancient province in what is now the Pas-de-Calais *département* of northern France) continues to flow because it is constantly being fed with water draining through the aquifer. Once drilled, it is very reliable.

Above the confining layer, a second aquifer can form if there is sufficient depth of soil. This is a *perched aquifer* and, because it lies at a shallower depth it is often easier to tap. It can also happen that one impermeable layer is so far below the one above it that the aquifer between them never fills with water. Although it is sealed, it is unconfined. It is possible, therefore, for one unconfined aquifer to lie directly above another.

Aquifers hold vast stores of water, but they are not inexhaustible. If water is taken from them faster than precipitation can recharge them, they will be depleted. Water tables have fallen in many parts of the world because of the rate at which groundwater has been abstracted.

How droughts are classified

A few weeks without rain in summer and Britain suffers a drought. Officially, a British drought is a period of 15 consecutive days without rain. People are forbidden to use garden hoses and lawn sprinklers, and car washes close. The U.S. Weather Bureau defines a drought as a period of 21 or more days during which rainfall is no more than 30% of the average for that particular place and time of year. In parts of North Africa, a drought occurs when no rain has fallen for at least two years. In Egypt, before the Aswan Dam regulated its flow, a drought year was one in which the Nile failed to flood farmlands downstream and in the river delta. In India, there is a drought if the summer monsoon brings only half the usual amount of rain.

All of these are droughts, but they are very different and so are their consequences. In Britain a drought most obviously means brown lawns, wilting flowers, and dirty cars. It sounds trivial, but drought can also reduce water supplies to industry, leading to factory closures and unemployment, and it reduces yields of most farm crops, sometimes drastically. Elsewhere in the world, drought can mean starvation.

Clearly, defining just what we mean by "drought" is not simple. It is not enough to say it is a period without rain, or with less rain than is usual, because it may follow a period of high rainfall. Reservoirs may be full and the water table high, so the lack of rain brings no shortages and plants grow vigorously in the bright sunshine. Perhaps, then, it is a period during which rainfall is insufficient to meet the needs of plants. This is better, but plants vary widely in their requirements. Cabbages need a lot more water than cacti.

Since cabbages and cacti grow naturally in very different climates, the first step in deciding whether or not a period of dry weather constitutes a drought is to consider those climates. This approach identifies four types of drought.

The first is *permanent*. It is the drought of deserts, where farmers can grow crops only on irrigated land. Except after the very rare, but often heavy rains, there are no rivers or streams.

Seasonal drought, the second type, is less extreme, but no less predictable. It occurs in climates where all the rain, or almost all of it, falls during one season. Most plants native to such regions germinate and grow during the rainy season and survive the dry season as seeds or in a dormant state. San Diego, California, for example, has an average 10.2 inches of rain a year, but 74% of it falls in winter, from December to March. Bombay, India, has an average 71.3 inches of rain a year and 94% of it falls between June and September, during the summer monsoon.

Devastating droughts are of the third type. These are the droughts no one can predict. Some accident of nature causes the rain to fail. It can happen anywhere, at any time, without warning, and its end is no easier to predict than its start. If the drought occurs in winter most people may be hardly aware of it because that is not the growing season for plants, but if it occurs in summer plants wilt and die. This is a *contingent*, or *accidental*, drought.

A drought or near drought may cause water tables and the water level in streams and rivers to fall and the soil becomes very dry. The drought may seem to end with the arrival of rain showers, but this is a fourth type of drought, an *invisible* one, and it is troublesome. Rain does fall, but when the amount of water lost by evaporation and transpiration is deducted, what remains is insufficient to recharge the aquifers. River levels and water tables remain low, and plants, especially crop plants, continue to suffer. A drought of this kind is troublesome because many people refuse to believe it exists. They cannot see why they should economize in their use of water when rain showers are fairly frequent, so public demand, which was reduced during the "visible" drought, slowly increases.

It was the American meteorologists C. W. Thornthwaite and J. R. Mather who divided droughts into these four types in 1955 in the course of developing a system for classifying climates. There have been many attempts to classify climates, and the one Thornthwaite devised in 1931 (see *A Chronology of Weather* for more details) and greatly improved in 1948 is widely used.

The Thornthwaite classification is partly based on *potential evapotranspiration* (*PE*). This is calculated from the average monthly temperature, corrected for day length, and represents the amount of water that could be lost by evapotranspiration were there no water shortage at all. Once the *PE* value is known it can be combined with the amount of annual precipitation (*r*) to calculate a *moisture index* (*Im*) by the equation $Im = 100(r/PE - 1)$. The moisture index allows the severity of droughts to be compared and is similar to the equation (r/t), which uses average annual precipitation (*r*) and temperature (*t*) to define the aridity of climates (see page 11).

Droughts of the past

Hurricanes, typhoons, and floods cause widespread devastation and often kill large numbers of people. Blizzards disrupt communications. All are terrible, terrifying events, but they pass and the survivors recover. Droughts are different. They can destroy empires and change the course of history. They have done so several times.

Around 2500 B.C., Akkad was the biggest and most powerful empire in the world. At its height, under its ruler Sargon, in about 2300 B.C., Akkad controlled the trade in valuable materials from Turkey to Afghanistan and south to the Gulf of Oman. In Mesopotamia, the land between the rivers Tigris and Euphrates in territory now forming part of Syria and Iraq, fortresses were built to guard the wheat fields and irrigation canals dug to supply water to the crops. The Akkadian capital was a great city covering more than 200 acres, with fine buildings, paved streets, and drains to carry away surplus water. On the Syrian plain where that fine city once stood there is now a large sand dune, called Tell Leilan, burying all that remains of it.

For the Akkadians, everything started to go wrong in about 2200 B.C. They had captured the city at Tell Leilan and expanded it, but in less than a century they abandoned it. Between 2200 and 1900 B.C. people moved away from that entire region in great numbers. The rains had become irregular and then they failed, and the wheat fields were buried beneath windblown sand. For a century or more the drought continued and the center of the first great empire in the world turned into desert. Akkad collapsed.

The Akkadians were not the only ones to suffer, for the drought was very extensive. Between 2200 and 2100 B.C., towns were abandoned in Palestine, as were Mohenjo-daro and Harappa in the Indus Valley. The civilizations of Crete and Greece failed and a marked decrease in the amount of water flowing in the Nile coincided with the collapse of the Old Kingdom of ancient Egypt.

No one knows what caused the drought or why it lasted for so long, but there is strong evidence that it occurred and was widespread. In time, of course, new civilizations and empires arose to replace those that had vanished, but had drought not cleared away old empires, and perhaps old ideas, ancient history might have developed quite differently from the way it did.

Drought has also influenced Asian history. In about A.D. 300 there was severe drought in central Asia, which recurred at intervals throughout the fourth century. Examination of sediments shows a fall in the water level of the Caspian Sea at that time, and there are remains of settlements abandoned then in various parts of central Asia and northern China. At times, water and grazing were so scarce that it became impossible for camel caravans to travel the great Silk Road by which exotic luxuries from China had been reaching the west since the route opened in about 150 B.C.

All of this happened just as nomadic peoples were fighting the Chinese to the south, possibly because they needed pasture for their animals, their traditional grazing lands having become too parched and eroded to supply the feed they needed. The nomads invaded northern China and the resulting conflict brought about the collapse of the Tsin dynasty. Refugees fled from the war, moving south and east, into southern China, Korea, and Japan. There they stimulated the development of culture and introduced a strong Chinese influence. It may be that the present cultures of Korea and Japan owe much to that drought some 1,700 years ago.

Europe did not remain untouched. The same drought that drove the expansion of the nomadic peoples to the south may also have been what drove them westward. In about 370 B.C. the Hunni people, or Huns, invaded southeastern Europe, defeating every army that tried to halt them until they reached the border of the Roman Empire at the Danube. Their most famous king was Attila, who was known as the "Scourge of God." He was born much later and ruled from 434 to 453 (his year of birth is not known). The Romans paid tribute (taxes) to him and his ceaseless pressure on them contributed to the fall of the Roman Empire. If it was the central

Asian droughts which destroyed pastures and sent these magnificent horsemen and fearsome archers westward in the fourth century, those droughts had far-reaching consequences.

Investigations by archeologists, geologists, and paleoclimatologists (scientists who reconstruct what ancient climates were like) led them to realize what had happened to Akkad, but most droughts are not studied so closely. One exception is a very long drought that affected the southwestern part of what is now the United States. It began in 1246, reached its greatest severity from 1276 to 1299, and the rains did not return with any regularity until 1305. America is no stranger to droughts, of course. Since the first Europeans arrived and started recording them, they have returned to the Middle West fairly regularly at intervals of 20 to 22 years (see page 76).

In most cases, however, what little we know of ancient droughts is pieced together from records made at the time. Harvest records are useful, because they have always been important and often include information about the weather during the growing season. Unfortunately, they are incomplete, with long periods for which records have been lost. They do reveal that a drought in England lasted from A.D. 678 to 681 and that there was another from 1276 to 1278, but that is all they tell.

More is known about two droughts that affected England in the 14th century. One in 1305 was serious enough to cause the failure of the grass crop being grown for hay. This led to the starvation of many farm animals and also of humans, although the famine coincided with a smallpox epidemic. There is no way to separate famine deaths from those caused by disease, but almost certainly one would have contributed to the other, because people weakened by hunger would have had less resistance to infection. Famine returned in 1353. The drought of that year lasted from March until the end of July, and rainfall remained low and the ground dry into the following year.

The early years of the 14th century marked the beginning of a major climatic change. Until the Middle Ages Europe had enjoyed a "climatic optimum" in which average temperatures were relatively high. In England, summer temperatures were 1.25–1.8° F warmer than they are today, and in central Europe the difference was even more marked. Cereal crops were grown in Norway and Iceland, and England was a major wine producer. Then, after 1300, the climate started to cool rapidly. Average temperatures continued to fall until about 1700, after which they began a slow recovery that may still be continuing. This cold period is known as the Little Ice Age. Its effects were complex, but most historians believe the disappearance of English wine production during the 14th century was at least partly due to repeated failures of the grape harvest, which made English vineyards uneconomic compared with those of the Bordeaux region. France did not escape its share of the climatic turmoil of those centuries. In the 1650s there was drought lasting several years in the Midi, in central France. It was so serious in 1654 that in August the people of Périgueux, in the Dordogne, made a formal visit to the shrine containing the relics of St. Sabina to ask her to intervene and bring rain.

Although the Little Ice Age brought low average temperatures, it also brought extremes. There were extremely cold winters and cool summers, but also mild winters and very hot summers and the weather fluctuated between them very rapidly. In the winter of 1683–84, for example, the average temperature in central England was 37° F and the following winter, of 1685–86, it was 50.5° F. The summers of 1665 and 1666 were very hot. The first year brought the last outbreak of plague ever to affect England and one of the most serious. It began in the winter, but was firmly established by summer and by the end of the year nearly 69,000 people had died from it.

The following year, 1666, also brought a hot, dry summer over much of Europe. At London, the level of water in the Thames fell so low that the boatmen who earned their livings ferrying goods and people were threatened with ruin. There was simply not enough water for them to ply their trade. Samuel Pepys, the diarist, wrote that the drought had continued so long that "even the stones were ready to burst into flames." Not that most of the buildings in London were made from stone. They were of wood, and were dry as tinder. On September 2 a small fire broke out in the house of a baker near London Bridge. It spread rapidly and blazed out of control for four days. When it died down four-fifths of the buildings in the city had been destroyed, and so had the unsanitary conditions that had favored the rats that were spreading plague. This was the Great Fire of London. After it, the city was rebuilt, this time in brick and stone. The drought of 1666 may not have changed history on a very large scale, but it certainly altered the way London developed, and it brought an end to plague in England.

Hot summers returned a decade later and brought repeated droughts in France between 1676 and 1686. Springs dried as water tables fell and in 1686 the Midi was invaded by grasshoppers migrating from the south. Then, some years later, it was the turn of England again. A drought began in 1730 and lasted until June of 1734.

Much of North Africa lies within the Sahara, a name derived from the Arabic *as-Sahra*, meaning the "waste" or "wilderness." It is desert, where drought is permanent. It was not always so. Until about 4000 B.C., there were grasslands and herds of animals grazing them; the water level in Lake Chad, even earlier a large inland sea, was still about 130 feet higher than it is today. Much later than that, empires flourished further south. One of these, centered on Timbuktu, was the Mandingo Empire of Mali. Its merchants traded over a wide area, spreading the religion of Islam as they did so. By the 16th century their influence was declining, and at the same time the climate was becoming drier. Timbuktu lies near the river Niger, where the river curves through a large bend to the north. The city has been flooded many times, but it has also suffered from drought, sometimes in the same years as the floods. Between 1617 and 1743 drought repeatedly caused famine. It was the time of the Little Ice Age and the northward movement of the intertropical convergence in summer was reduced. Until then, that northward movement had brought summer rains. Now the rains often failed. It was not the change in climate that caused the collapse of the Mali Empire in 1591 so much as internal dissention and a Moroccan invasion, but drought may have contributed to its weakness and to the failure of the invaders to establish an empire to replace it.

Mali lies within the region now known as the Sahel, on the southern border of the Sahara proper. Drought in the Sahel in the late 1960s and early 1970s was one of the most serious of modern times (see page 81), but the Sahel was not the only region to be afflicted. By the summer of 1972, when the seasonal rains failed to materialize in the highlands of Ethiopia, it was clear the drought had spread into East Africa. Cereal crops could not be planted in the worst affected areas the following spring, and by May around 80% of the cattle and some camels had died in Welo and Tigray regions and parts of Shewa region. By September, somewhere between 100,000 and 150,000 people had died.

Realization of the extent and complete chaos of the catastrophe probably contributed to the revolt against the feudal regime which

Figure 21: *Between wheat and cotton fields, water flows downhill from a pumping station of the Rharb Valley irrigation project in Morocco, 1973.* (UN photo 133625/Bill Graham)

began in February, with widespread strikes in the capital, Addis Ababa. Troops sided with the strikers and on September 12 the government was overthrown. The revolution and civil war which followed it did little to relieve the drought and famine. The rains started to return in June 1975, by which time Ogaden, in the south, was the most seriously striken part of the country and there and in the neighboring part of Somalia some 40,000 people died, but suffering continued through most of 1976. A few years later, the rains failed once more. This time the effects of the drought were exacerbated by war in the Ogaden region between Ethiopian and Somali guerrillas and between Ethiopian and Eritrean forces in Tigray, in the north.

Morocco also suffered from drought in 1980 and 1981, which forced the government to import food. The cost of the imports caused serious economic difficulties and in 1982 Morocco had to borrow $579 million through the International Monetary Fund in order to buy food. On the other side of the world, Australia was also suffering severe drought. By September the government was having to pay huge sums to help farmers survive.

Like North Africa, large parts of Australia have a dry climate. Droughts are common and must be unusually prolonged before their effects become really serious. Australians take ground water from wells thousands of feet deep (see page 62) and know how to cope. People living in equatorial regions, where rainfall is heavy and ordinarily reliable, do not expect drought, but even there it can happen. Some parts of Indonesia receive more rainfall than others, but nowhere is the climate dry. Jakarta, the capital, has an average 70 inches of rain a year, and it is not the wettest place in the country. Nevertheless, in 1982, a drought in Indonesia lasted for four months. The drought did not cause famine, but water supplies were contaminated and in October more than 150 people died from cholera (caused by bacteria and spread through infected food and water) and dengue fever (caused by a virus transmitted by mosquitoes, which breed in stagnant water). It seems likely that the 1982 Indonesian drought was linked to the ENSO event (see page 36) occurring at the same time.

Droughts are not like other natural disasters. Those are events that pass, allowing people to rebuild their lives and homes. Droughts do not pass so quickly. Once the aquifers dry out below ground, the flow of water to lakes and rivers slows and then ceases. The drought bites deep into the land and there can be no full recovery from it until the aquifers have been recharged. It is not enough for rain to fall, even if it falls heavily. The rain must continue long enough to soak the ground so that water can drain downward and restore the lost groundwater. Then, as the aquifers resume their slow transport of water, there will be a delay before that water reaches the rivers. It is a process that cannot take less than months and often takes a year or more, even in those parts of the world which enjoy a mild, wet climate. In England, for example, the drought caused by prolonged dry, hot weather in the summer of 1995 continued through the winter because rainfall was somewhat lower than usual and depleted aquifers and reservoirs fed from rivers did not refill sufficiently to provide for the anticipated needs of the following summer, when rising temperatures would increase the rate of surface evaporation. If that is the effect in cool, damp Britain, imagine how much more serious drought can be in hot, dry Africa or Australia.

Drought and soil erosion

On a dry day in summer, the sky is often a pale shade of blue, sometimes almost white. Then there is a heavy shower, and when the shower ends the air feels fresher and the sky is a much deeper blue. The whiteness of the sky in dry weather is due to dust particles. These are tiny, about 0.00002 to 0.0004 inch in diameter, but there can be 30 or more of them in every cubic inch of clean, country air and in air dusty enough to make the sky white there are many more.

If the Earth had no atmosphere, the Sun would be very bright, but the sky would be black. We see a bright sky because particles in the air scatter the sunlight, making it reach us from all directions. The way light is scattered depends on the size of the particles off which it bounces in relation to the wavelength of the light. The diameter of an air molecule is about one-tenth the wavelength of light, and air molecules scatter the shorter waves more than the longer ones. Blue light is at the shortwave end of the light spectrum, so if the light is being scattered by air molecules it is mainly blue light that reaches us from all directions, making the sky blue. Small though they are, dust particles are much bigger and scatter all wavelengths equally, so the light we see is white, composed of all wavelengths.

Rain clears the air, and changes the color of the sky by washing the dust particles to the ground, but during a drought there is no rain and dust particles accumulate. They can travel great distances in very dry air. Two or three times in most years southerly winds carry dust from the Sahara all the way to Britain, 1,600 miles away, where showers wash it to the ground. The Saharan dust is red and if there is enough of it the rain is blood-red and afterwards everything is covered with a thin coating of red dust. During World War II, tank battles in North Africa raised so much dust it colored clouds over the Caribbean. Scientists have calculated that a dust storm covering 5,000 square miles to a height of 10,000 feet can carry up to 7 million tons of dust.

Most atmospheric dust consists of soil particles. Some have been thrown into the air by human activity. Watch a farmer plowing dry soil and you will see how much dust this raises. Driving along dirt roads raises dust. So, of course, do tank battles. Wind alone can raise dust. You can see this on any windy day in dry weather.

No matter how it happens, once soil particles have been carried aloft they are transported from the place where they were picked up and deposited somewhere else. They are lost from their original site. The loss of soil is called *erosion* and the amount is considerable. The most famous example in modern times happened in the 1930s, in the area which came to be known as the Dust Bowl (see page 76), but there are others. In 1977, blowing soil caused damage and severe erosion over an area of about 750 square miles in the San Joaquin Valley, California. Within 24 hours more than 25 million tons of soil was carried away from grazing land, and the same drought also caused severe erosion on the High Plains of Texas. It is true, of course, that when soil is blown away from the surface of the land it falls again somewhere else, but this does not necessarily mean that one farmer's loss is another's gain. Much of the blown soil may be carried over the sea, and soil that does fall on farmland is not welcome there. It buries crops that have just germinated; coats leaves with fine particles, which damages them; clogs ditches; and blocks roads.

In some places, however, the wind has delivered very fertile soils, called *loess*. Large areas on the northeast and east banks of the Mississippi and Missouri rivers have deep loess soils. They are also found in the Rhine basin, in Europe, in the valley of the Hwang Ho (Yellow River) in China, and in various other parts of Europe, Russia, and South America. These soils were blown to their present locations when the ice sheets retreated at the end of the last ice age. Meltwaters carried fine soil particles and deposited them as sediments. Then the climate dried and the soils blew. Unfortunately, of course, they are still capable of being blown.

Soil particles stick together when they are wet. A film of water covers each of them and the water molecules on adjacent particles are linked by their hydrogen bonds. Even beach sand grains will hold together in this way, if only weakly because of the large size of the particles. You can build sand castles in damp sand, but they collapse when the sand dries. Very dry sand, on the other hand, will blow in the wind and small sandstorms can and do happen on coastal beaches.

Only dry soil will blow away in the wind. This means that those parts of the world where the climate is dry, with less than 12 inches of rain a year, are the most vulnerable to soil erosion by wind. Predictably, desert areas are most at risk, indicated in figure 22, but

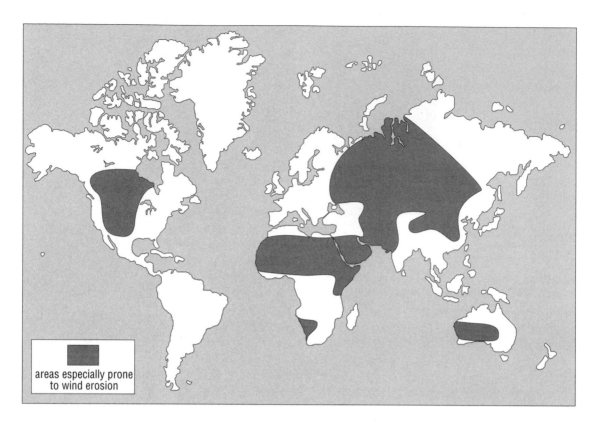

areas especially prone
to wind erosion

Figure 22: *Parts of the world where the risk of wind erosion is high.*

wind erosion is not confined to deserts and semi-arid regions. It can happen anywhere. If the rainfall occurs mainly at one time of year, at other times the soil surface may be very dry. Even if the rainfall is ordinarily distributed evenly through the year, a contingent drought (see page 65) can dry the soil.

Obviously, the smaller the soil particles are, the lower the wind speed that is needed to detach them. The likelihood that a dry soil will be eroded by the wind therefore depends on the size of its particles and the strength of the wind. It also depends on the roughness of the ground surface. A rough surface, littered with large stones or clods of soil, slows the wind by friction. This reduces the amount of erosion. Vegetation also reduces wind erosion, partly by increasing the roughness of the surface and partly because plant roots tend to bind soil particles together.

Once a particle has been lifted from the ground it will start to fall again, and the speed with which it falls is related to its diameter. The smallest particles, up to 0.0004 inch in diameter, fall so slowly they can be caught and lifted further by eddies and remain airborne for days. These are the particles that travel long distances and cause "blood rain" in Britain. The particles become suspended in the air, and of all the particles moved by wind erosion, wind-tunnel experiments have shown between 3% and 38% travel in this fashion.

The biggest particles are not lifted from the ground at all. This is called *creep* erosion. Too big to be lifted, they are rolled along the ground. In principle there is no limit to how big these particles might be, but in practice most are no more than 0.08 inch across. Watch a light breeze blowing over the surface of dry sand and you will see grains being rolled along in this way. Between 7% and 25% of particles travel by creep.

Most—about 55–72% of all eroded particles—move by *saltation*, literally in leaps and bounds. The wind lifts the particle clear of the surface. It starts to fall again immediately, but the wind is still pushing it forward and accelerating it. It rises no further than an inch or two, but travels a forward distance approximately equal to ten times the height it reaches, and when it strikes the ground it does so with considerable force. This knocks loose another particle, which leaps forward to dislodge a third, and so the process continues, with the dislodged particles falling, dislodging more particles, then being lifted again themselves.

Although fine particles can be carried to a great height, saltation is by far the most important factor in wind erosion and it occurs within a few inches, or at most a few feet, of the surface. It can produce a kind of dust or sand storm so shallow that people can walk through it with their heads and shoulders in clear air and the

Figure 23: *A dust storm whips across the landscape at Opuwo, Namibia, 1989.* (UN photo 157109/Milton Grant)

Soil erodibility

The vulnerability of a particular soil to wind erosion is calculated from the wind erodibility equation, devised by W. S. Chepil and N. P. Woodruff in 1963. The equation is: $E = f(I, K, C, L, V)$, where E is the total erosion loss in tons of soil per year; f indicates that erosion is a function of the listed items; I is the soil erodibility index based on particle size and the extent to which particles adhere to one another; K is surface roughness; C is the climate factor, based on wind speed and effective moisture in the soil; L is "field length", which is the distance across which the wind blows; and v is a value for the type of vegetation.

The calculation is usually performed by specialized computer software. Before this was available, the complicated calculation produced an estimated value that was used to read the final value from a published graph.

lower parts of their bodies invisible in the swirling cloud. Within a height of 3.3 feet, a wind of 18 MPH can shift 490 pounds of sand in an hour from a strip of land one foot wide and a 25-MPH wind can move 990 pounds an hour. Imagine a square plot of land with an area of one acre and the 25-MPH wind is blowing about 60 tons of soil out of it every hour.

Estimating the vulnerability of a particular area to wind erosion is complicated, but possible and very important to farmers. Scientists measure the size of the soil particles, the roughness of the surface, and the area of land exposed, take account of the rainfall and wind, and feed the data into computers. Specialized software programs then calculate the risk of erosion from the "wind erodibility equation" devised in 1963 by two soil scientists, W. S. Chepil and N. P. Woodruff (see box)

This is a complicated task, but possible values for one of the factors in the equation give an idea of the scale of risk. *Erodibility* is the vulnerability of a soil to erosion when dry. It is calculated by sieving a measured volume of soil to determine the percentage of particles larger than 0.84 mm (0.03 inch) in diameter. Standard tables then show the erodibility of that soil in tons per acre. If 5% of particles are more than 0.84 mm in size, the soil can lose 180 tons per acre, and if 50% of them are more than 0.84 mm it can lose 38 tons per acre.

The Dust Bowl

Inside the White House in May 1934, dust settled on the desk of the president and as fast as it was cleaned away, more collected. Outside, in New York and Baltimore as well as in Washington, the sky was so dark with clouds of dust that in some places chickens roosted, thinking it was night. Dust settled on ships, 300 miles out

Figure 24: Area affected in the Dust Bowl years.

at sea. Ducks and geese fell from the sky, choked to death by the dust through which they flew. People called the storms "black blizzards." At their height, a single dust cloud 3 miles high covered 1.35 million square miles, from Canada to Texas and Montana to Ohio.

All the dust was soil, blown from farmlands covering 150,000 square miles in southwestern Kansas, southeastern Colorado, northeastern and southeastern New Mexico, and the panhandles of Oklahoma and Texas. Figure 24 shows how large an area was affected. This region, the source of the black blizzards and where soil was blown into dunes in places 30 feet high, came to be known as the Dust Bowl.

Before the first European farmers arrived, the Great Plains of North America were prairie grassland. Grasses were the commonest plants, some growing as tussocks of grass more than 3 feet tall. Grasses bind soil and prevent wind erosion. The tall tussocks slow the ground-level wind, and grass roots form a mat with soil held among the fibers. The climate is fairly dry and very windy. Boise City, in northwest Oklahoma, has an average annual rainfall of 16.5

inches and Dodge City, Kansas, 20.4 inches. Grassland vegetation is well adapted to a fairly low annual rainfall and occasional drought.

To the settlers arriving from the east, the grasslands were deceptive. Many were drawn to the plains by the Homestead Act of 1862, which offered free land to people willing to farm it. To them, the prairies looked much like eastern grasslands, which grow in a much wetter climate. The farmers cleared the natural vegetation by burning it repeatedly and plowed up the grasslands to grow wheat. When there was rain the soil was fertile and the harvests were good, but from time to time drought caused the crops to fail. Farmers were ruined and abandoned their land and homes. A year or two later the rains returned, the land was plowed again, and new homes were built.

So it continued until around 1915. Plowing and harrowing with horses was slow, hard work, but it was about then that the first tractors rolled onto the prairies. They made it much easier to till the land. Between 1910 and 1919 the area growing wheat in Kansas increased from less than 5 million acres to more than 12 million acres, an increase achieved by plowing more of the natural prairie. Then the combine harvester was introduced to speed harvesting.

The machines were expensive, of course, but by 1919 wheat prices were rising to pay for them. Farming was highly profitable and becoming less arduous year by year. The pioneer farmers of the 19th century had struggled to break a land full of tough clods of soil, but eventually the battle was won and the soil worked into a fine, friable texture that was exactly the condition needed for sowing seeds.

Figure 25: A farmer examines his field during the Dust Bowl. (Archive photos)

All went well for several years, but then the national economy crashed and the Great Depression of the twenties and thirties began. Cereal prices fell, forcing the prairie farmers to work the land even more intensively to maintain their incomes by producing more grain. Little by little farming incomes fell until the poorest farmers were in a desperate position. The weather was still favorable, however, so the farms remained productive. Between 1927 and 1933 the annual rainfall was 5 inches above average in Nebraska, Iowa, and Kansas.

Far away on the other side of the Atlantic, certain changes were becoming noticeable. At Spitsbergen, inside the Arctic Circle, there is a port from which coal was exported. Prior to 1920 it was free of ice for three months of the year, but each year it remained accessible just a little longer. By 1940 it was open for more than seven months each year. Over the entire northern hemisphere, the climate was becoming warmer. One consequence of this climatic change was a marked increase in the number of days when westerly winds blew in middle latitudes. Lands on the eastern side of oceans received more rainfall because they were exposed more frequently to winds carrying moisture collected at sea.

That is not what happened in the prairies. There, westerly winds blowing across the Pacific lost their moisture as they crossed the Rockies, so the winds reaching the prairie farms were very dry. Rainfall that had been above average fell to 16 inches, 7 inches below the average 23 inches a year. Crops began to fail and the remaining natural prairie grasses began to die back. As vegetation disappeared, the soil was left bare.

Rainfall had always been highly variable and in dry periods the natural grasses would disappear. Their mats of roots used to remain, binding the soil into the tough clods that gave the farmers so much trouble, and the clods would bake hard in the dry heat. Now tilled to a fine texture by farmers and dried by the drought, the soil began to blow. The most severe dust storms were in May 1934 and October 1935, but the loss of soil was almost continuous. Already weakened economically by the depression, countless farmers were ruined and migrated with their families, most of them to California. The Dust Bowl drought continued from 1933 until the winter of 1940–41, when the rains returned and the native grasses started to recover.

The experience of the Dust Bowl led to the formation of the Soil Conservation Service in 1935, and the federal government started to teach and promote throughout the nation farming techniques that protect the soil. Even so, when grain prices rise, prairie lands are plowed once again.

This was neither the first nor the last severe drought to afflict the plains. Writing in the fall of 1830, Isaac McCoy, an explorer in what is now part of Kansas, described fierce storms of dust, sand, and ash from the recently burned grasslands. The Republican River, he wrote on October 27, "runs over a bed of sand—the banks low, and

Figure 26: *A Dust Bowl family.* (Archive photos)

all the bottom lands are a bed of sand white and fine, and now as dry as powder ought to be." On November 5 there was another storm. "It was not three minutes after I had discovered its approach, before the sun was concealed, and the darkness so great, that I could not distinguish objects more than three or four times the length of my horse."

The droughts tend to occur at intervals of 20 to 23 years, some more severe than others. Erosion, dust storms, and ruined crops returned to the plains in the 1950s, but the 1970s were especially harsh. Late in February 1977, a storm lasting 24 hours in eastern Colorado produced winds of 90 MPH. It stripped away about 5 tons of soil from every acre of farmland. From Nebraska to the panhandles of Oklahoma and Texas there were dust clouds at times 12,000 feet thick, and visibility was reduced almost to zero.

Then, in the 1990s, the rains failed again. In the winter of 1995–96 there were record snowfalls over the eastern states and in the Rockies, but in Kansas, Oklahoma, and Texas the plains remained dry. Between October and May, San Antonio, Texas, expects 15.8 inches of rain. In the period of 1994–95 it received 4 inches, and in 1995–96, 3.7 inches fell. Winter wheat died. This is the crop sown in late fall to germinate just before winter sets in, then resume its growth in spring to produce a bigger harvest than spring-sown wheat. Such crops as survived yielded harvests less than half of normal. The pastures failed and there was a shortage of cattle feed. By May 1996, 40% of Texas was too dry to be grazed and farmers were selling their cattle at auctions that had to continue through the night to cope with the numbers. Shortages caused grain prices to

Figure 27: *A farmer in Iowa with a stunted soybean crop during the drought of 1988.* (U.S. Department of Agriculture)

double and animals were selling for less than the price of one ton of feed. Four out of five of the cows were pregnant. This meant farmers could not afford even to wait until the calves were born and sell two head instead of one. Of the 70,000 farmers in Oklahoma, it was estimated that between 7% and 14% would go bankrupt during 1996.

Windbreaks and shelter belts have been planted, as well as grasses to bind the soil. This time the drought did not darken the noonday sky with blowing soil, but the catastrophe was no less severe for rural communities than those following previous droughts.

No one knows why drought returns to the Great Plains at such regular intervals. The interval, of 20 to 23 years, coincides more or less with the solar cycle. Solar radiation varies in intensity, reaching a maximum about every 11 years and indicated by *sunspots*, which are dark patches on the surface of the Sun. Solar output is greatest when there are most sunspots and this variation may affect the climates of the Earth indirectly. The difference in output between solar maxima and minima is only about 0.1%, but most of this variation is in ultraviolet radiation, rather than visible light or heat. Ultraviolet radiation is absorbed in the ozone layer of the stratosphere, which warms the stratosphere and slightly alters the atmospheric circulation in the troposphere. Some scientists think this might be enough to trigger ENSO episodes (see page 36) and possibly the periodic droughts of the Great Plains. If they are right, it may be possible in years to come to forecast major climatic events of this kind far in advance because the activity of the Sun can be predicted fairly accurately.

Such knowledge will not prevent drought, but if farmers are prepared at least they may escape the personal tragedies it causes.

The Sahel

In 1972 the total amount of food produced throughout the world was the second highest ever, but it fell 2% short of the 1971 output. World production had been rising steadily since 1945, usually by about 3% a year, but in 1972 it suffered its first reverse. In Russia the 1972 grain harvest was 13% below the amount that had been predicted; in Australia the wheat crop was 25% below the average of the previous 5 years; the coffee harvest failed in Ethiopia, Kenya, and Côte d'Ivoire; the peanut, sorghum, and rice crops failed in Nigeria; and an El Niño drastically reduced the Peruvian fish catch (see page 38). Apart from the failure of the Peruvian fisheries, all of the decline in crop yields was due to heat and drought.

There were widespread repercussions. Countries that needed to increase their imports of food looked to the large reserves held by the United States. Russia got there first, buying up one-quarter of them and then buying still more from other countries that had surpluses. Rising demand caused wheat prices to double in a matter of months, and those countries with abundant oil but a desert climate suddenly realized that food is important and one day their oil fields would be empty. To secure their future they raised oil prices. In 1973 and 1974 the world price of oil increased fourfold.

When prices suddenly increase in this way the poor suffer most. If they cannot afford the new price for oil, their factories may close, increasing unemployment, and there will be shortages of fuel for transport and essential services such as hospitals. Many countries lack sufficient reserves of foreign currencies to pay for the food imports they need and, even if they can pay, many of their people cannot afford the new, higher prices.

Of all the poor in the world, some of the very poorest live in the countries along the southern border of the Sahara Desert, in Mauritania, Mali, Burkina Faso, Niger, Chad, Sudan, and Ethiopia (see figure 28). To give an idea of the economic situation of these countries, the table below sets out the per capita gross national product for each country in 1995, in U.S. dollars, with that of the United States for comparison. *Gross national product*, or GNP, is the total value of all the goods and services produced in a country; *per capita* means per person living in that country.

Country	Per capita GNP (U.S.$)
Mauritania	438
Mali	300
Burkina Faso	300
Niger	270
Chad	200
Sudan	300
Ethiopia	100
United States	25,850

These are the countries of the Sahel region and it was their plight that caught the attention of the world in the 1970s as their lands were ravaged by a drought that probably began in the late 1960s and continued until the mid-1980s. Although it was the Sahel

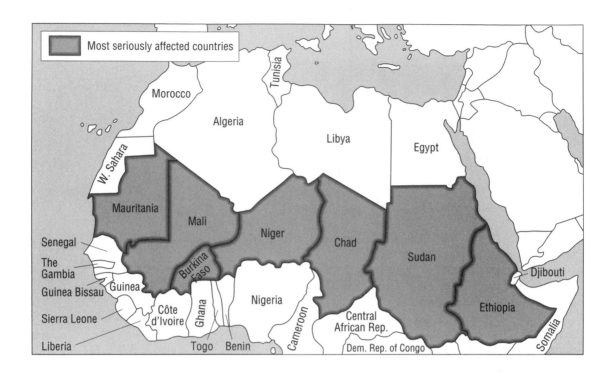

Figure 28: *The Sahel region of Africa.*

countries that were most seriously affected, the drought extended much farther. It was severe in Angola and Mozambique and most of East Africa was affected, as well as Senegal and Guinea Bissau in West Africa.

Except in small, scattered areas, lands near the edge of a desert cannot be cultivated. Rainfall is always too sparse and too unreliable for crops to grow, and the plants adapted to this climate are mainly grasses, herbs, and small, thorny shrubs. When it does rain they produce leaves and flourish, and between rains they lie dormant. The land cannot be farmed, but it is possible to earn a meager living from it as a pastoralist, a person who tends herds and flocks of animals, moving with them from one area of pasture and watering place to another. This is the seminomadic, traditional way of life for many people in the Sahel.

They had pursued this way of life for centuries and were accustomed to drought. Rainfall in this area has always been erratic. In the good years, more livestock animals survived and the herds and flocks increased, providing food and materials for the next bad year, and in places people tilled the land and grew crops, including cotton, some of which was exported to generate cash income.

This way of life began to change in the 1960s. As the countries of this region of Africa developed, veterinary care and medicines became available. Fewer animals died from disease, and their numbers increased. In the cities there were people rich enough to buy meat, and this market also encouraged pastoralists to increase livestock numbers. The newly independent countries needed to earn foreign currency, so the growing of crops for export was encouraged. Between them, Burkina Faso, Chad, Mali, Niger, and Senegal produced 22.7 million tons of cotton in 1961–62, and in 1983–84 they produced 154 million tons.

These changes brought a little prosperity, but at the price of increased vulnerability. When the rains failed, such pasture as remained was consumed more quickly, and because more animals were now grazing it, plants that might have survived were uprooted or trampled to death, leaving the ground bare. This is overgrazing. At the same time, cash crops had been grown on land that previously would have grown food, some of which would have been stored for future use. Now there were insufficient stores.

Because they had no choice, the pastoralists began to move in search of water and better grazing. Thousands crossed from Mauritania into Mali, others from Mali into Burkina Faso and Niger. More than a million people entered Côte d'Ivoire. This mass migration increased the pressure on the little pasture remaining and compelled governments to establish refugee camps. Despite all the efforts of governments within the region and the international community, the United Nations Environment Program has suggested that between 1974 and 1984 at least 500,000 people died in Africa as a direct consequence of the drought, and that between 1970 and 1990 possibly two or three times that number perished.

The changes of the 1960s were helped by a series of years when rainfall was reliable and relatively high. At Diourbel in central Senegal, for example, the average annual rainfall between 1940 and 1969 was 27.6 inches. In 1966 it was 27.9 inches and in 1967 31.9 inches, but in 1968 it was only 13.9 inches. Then it increased again, to 34.4 inches in 1969, only to fall to 23.3 inches in 1970, 26.1 inches in 1971, and 14.7 inches in 1972. At Podor in northern Senegal, close to the Mauritanian border, in 1972 rainfall was 3 inches, compared to the 1940–69 average of 13.2 inches, and 17 inches fell in 1969. In Niger, rainfall in 1970 was only one-quarter of the annual average in 1970 and less than half of it in 1972.

The drought did not start suddenly, with a single disastrous year, but gradually, with a sequence of years in which rainfall was lower than usual. It was not dry enough to cause great harm, but it was bad enough to lead to some overgrazing and the lowering of water tables. Although rainfall was much heavier in 1969, this was not enough to recharge the aquifers and bring about a recovery from the steady deterioration of the preceding years. By the time the drought became noticeably severe, both the groundwater and pasture were already depleted.

West Africa north of the tropics relies on the summer monsoon for much of its rain. People usually think of the monsoon as a season

Figure 29:   *People leaving a drought stricken area in Chad, 1984.* (UN photo 154290/John Isaac)

of heavy rain in India, but other parts of the world also have them, including the United States (see page 87). Over the Sahel region, between about 10° N and 20° N, warm, dry air is descending on the high-latitude side of the Hadley cell circulation (see box on page 8). Near the surface, the prevailing winds are the north easterly trades, but high above the surface, from around 10,000 feet all the way to the stratosphere, they are westerlies (blowing from west to east). Further north, the prevailing surface winds are also westerlies.

In some years, anticyclones become stationary for weeks on end in middle latitudes over the North Atlantic. Air masses and weather systems continue to drift from west to east, but these blocking highs (see page 47) refuse to budge to make way for them. They have to go around them to the north or south, taking their low-pressure weather systems with them. When blocking highs become established in winter and spring, they can divert the low-pressure systems south into the Mediterranean region. For people in northwest Europe, the weather is cold and usually dry, often with northerly winds. In southern Europe, the weather is cool and wet. These patterns persist until air spilling out from the blocking high weakens it and the normal movement of air establishes itself once more.

These are the conditions people experience living at ground level, but the effects extend into the upper atmosphere. The southward deflection of the low-pressure systems is also accompanied by a similar deflection of a branch of the upper westerlies.

When this happens, the northward movement of the intertropical convergence zone is restricted. This is where the trade winds from either side of the equator meet, and it moves north in the northern hemisphere spring and summer and south in the southern hemisphere spring and summer. As it moves it takes with it the equatorial rains, bringing them further north or south. In the northern hemisphere they reach to about 20° N, the latitude that separates the Sahel in the south from the Sahara in the north.

If its seasonal migration is checked, so it does not move so far or moves more slowly, the summer rains do not extend so far as usual or they arrive late. If they arrive late they will also be briefer than usual because at the end of summer the intertropical convergence zone begins moving toward the other hemisphere, and if the rains do not last so long there is less time for rain to fall and the total rainfall will be less than usual. When this happens, the Sahel will experience a dry year; several such years in succession will mean drought. Scientists do not know what causes blocking highs to form over the North Atlantic, but their consequences for weather in the Sahel are clearly understood.

Back in the 1970s, some people believed the tragedy of the Sahel was the fault of the people living there. They said that greed led the pastoral peoples to keep more livestock and this led to overgrazing of the sparse pastures, leaving the ground exposed to the heat of the Sun and the wind. The soil dried and blew, burying adjacent land and killing crops growing on it. In this way the Sahara was expanding to the south.

This was unfair, although partly true. Certainly overgrazing damages the land, but the drought was due to the failure of the rains, not to anything local people had done, and there was nowhere else for them to take their animals. The pastures would have been overgrazed even if there had been fewer livestock, and many of these people, who are among the poorest in the world, measure their wealth and social status by the number of animals they control. It is also true that sand and dry topsoil blown from the drought areas buried crops and more fertile soil on adjacent land, but this has always happened when there was drought in the Sahel. When the rains return, the land recovers in the area bordering the Sahel as well as in the Sahel itself.

Monsoons

From November to May, Bombay has a dry climate. The average total rainfall during all of those seven months, calculated from records going back 60 years, amounts to a mere 1.6 inches. Then, in June, the rain starts. Between June and October the city receives about 70 inches, July being the wettest month. The rain starts to ease in August and dies away altogether by the end of October. Meanwhile, the temperature hardly varies. It is above 80° F throughout the year, with an average January temperature of 83° F. May is the warmest month, just before the rains begin. Then the average temperature is 91° F.

People who live in middle or high latitudes, well outside the tropics, think of the difference between summer and winter mainly in terms of temperature. Winters are cold. We wear thicker clothes and turn on the heat. In summer we wear lighter clothes and open the windows or turn on air conditioners. Summer days are longer than winter days, and the farther from the equator the bigger the difference. This can lead us to suppose that people who live in the tropics, and especially those who live very close to the equator, experience no seasons at all. It is true, of course, that day length changes very little through the year, although there is some change and equatorial plants are quite sensitive to it. Like plants in higher latitudes, flowering for many is triggered by changes in day length, but the changes to which they respond are very small. High-latitude plants would not respond to them. It is also true that daytime temperatures change little through the year. The difference between

Figure 30: *This farmer winnowing rice in Uttar Pradesh, India, in 1976 demonstrates farming during the dry winter monsoon.* (UN photo 134119/C. Srinivasan)

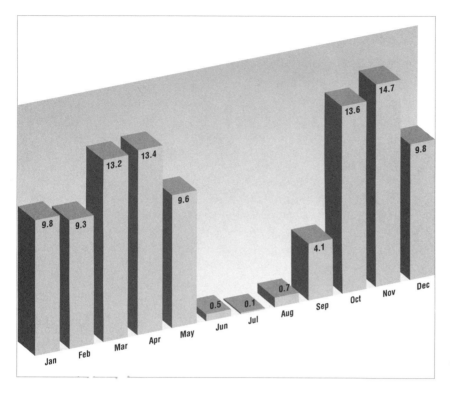

Figure 31: *Rainfall at Libreville (inches per month).*

the daytime and nighttime temperature is greater than that between "summer" and "winter" temperatures.

Add to this the idea (which is true) that rain forest is the natural kind of vegetation throughout most of the equatorial region, and we may suppose that rainfall is as constant as temperature. Rain forests, after all, grow in wet climates, where it rains heavily every day of the year. This is wrong. Libreville, for example is almost exactly on the equator (0°23' N) in Gabon, West Africa, and has an average annual rainfall of 98.8 inches, but, as figure 31 shows, the summers are dry, little more than 5% of the annual total falling between June and September. This is typical of much of the equatorial and tropical regions. There are seasons, but it is rainfall that makes summer and winter different, not temperature. At Libreville, the average daytime temperature ranges from 83° F in July to 89° F in March and April. So if you move to the tropics you will find people talk about the weather there, too!

The difference between the rainy and dry seasons is not usually so extreme as it is in Bombay, however. Bombay has a monsoon climate. The word *monsoon* was first used in the late 16th century by Dutch and Portuguese explorers who may have picked it up from an Arabic word, *mausim*, which means "season"; the English word has reached us from Dutch and Portuguese. All *monsoon* really means is "season," although we apply it to a special kind of season that is very strongly marked. We usually associate the monsoon with heavy rain, but this describes only one monsoon season and in fact there are two. The winter monsoon is dry and it is the summer monsoon that is wet.

The seasonal change occurs as the climatic equator (where temperature is highest) moves north and south of the geographic equator. As it moves it takes with it the belt of equatorial weather and extends the tropical and subtropical climate belts into higher latitudes. This is enough to produce seasons, but not to cause monsoons. They are due to the fact that there is much more land in the northern hemisphere than in the southern. This means that the subtropical region of high pressure and the low-pressure region in higher latitudes produced by the general circulation of the atmosphere (see box on page 90) are centered over land in one hemisphere and over sea in the other. This reverses the distribution of pressure from winter to summer and, with it, the direction of the prevailing wind.

In winter, the interior of the Asian continent lies beneath a shallow layer of cold, subsiding air. Pressure is high at the surface and the weather is dry. Above about 6,500 feet the winds blow from west to east, reaching a maximum force in the jet stream associated with the subtropical front (see page 43). The jet stream lies over the Himalayas at about 40,000 feet, but divides into two branches that reunite over northern China. The Tibetan Plateau rises to more than 13,000 feet over a huge area and India south of the Himalayas is very much warmer than Tibet, simply because of the difference in altitude. The average January daytime temperature in Lhasa, Tibet, is 44° F and in Delhi it is 70° F. This sharp decrease in temperature between south and north, combined with the barrier formed by the mountains, holds the southerly branch of the jet stream in position across northern India.

Air subsiding beneath the upper-level westerlies spills out from the Tibetan Plateau. Over the oceans to the south the maritime air is warmer and surface pressure lower. As the wind blows down from the mountains, at first it blows from the northwest, but by the time it reaches the Indian peninsula its direction is northeasterly. It blows across India and out across the sea. Because it originated in the dry interior of central Asia, the winds are also dry. This is the winter monsoon.

Early in spring the upper-level westerlies move away northward, but the jet stream remains in position across northern India, although it weakens. As the Sun moves north, temperatures rise. The weather grows very hot, and this causes a large area of low pressure to develop as warmed air rises by convection. Then the intertropical convergence, where the trade winds of both hemispheres meet, starts to move north across India. The jet stream weakens further, becomes intermittent, and finally shifts to the north of the Tibetan

Global circulation of the atmosphere

The tropics, of Cancer in the north and Capricorn in the south, mark the boundaries of the belt around the Earth where the Sun is directly overhead at noon on at least one day in the year. The Arctic and Antarctic Circles mark the boundaries of regions in which the Sun does not rise above the horizon on at least one day of the year and does not sink below the horizon on at least one day in the year.

Imagine a beam of sunlight just a few degrees wide. As the drawing shows, this beam illuminates a much smaller area if the Sun is

Global Distribution of pressure.

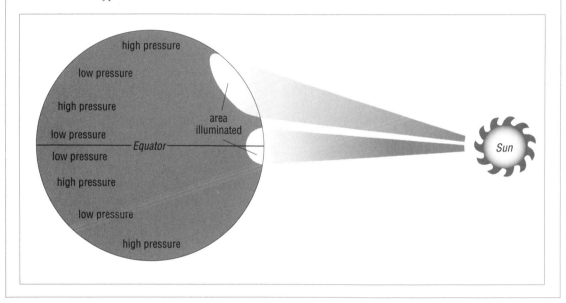

Plateau. South of the plateau the winds above about 20,000 feet become easterly and the low-level winds blow from the southwest. These are the southern-hemisphere trade winds. While they remain south of the equator they blow from the southeast, but in the northern hemisphere the Coriolis effect (see the box on page 32) swings them to the right, so as the intertropical convergence moves north, the winds on its southern side become southwesterly. They flow all the way across India, but are blocked when they reach the Himalayas. There they swing again until they are blowing from east to west and then north to south, carrying air back over the sea.

As trade winds, they already held a considerable amount of moisture. Now they approach India across the Arabian Sea, which the early summer sunshine has warmed to more than 80° F, and they collect still more. As they rise over the edge of the central Indian plateau the air cools, clouds form, and the rains begin. This is the summer monsoon, with its torrential rains. It ends with the fall, when directly overhead than it does if the Sun is at a low angle in the sky. The amount of energy in each beam is the same because they are of the same width, so energy is spread over a smaller area directly beneath the Sun than it is when the Sun is lower. This is why the tropics are heated more strongly than any other part of the Earth and the amount of heat we receive from the Sun decreases the further we are from the equator.

Solar energy warms the surface of land and water. The air is warmed by contact with the surface. As it is warmed, the air expands. This makes it less dense than the air immediately above it, so it rises, its place near the surface being taken by denser air flowing inward. This air is heated in its turn.

Where the surface is heated strongly and air in contact with it is expanding, there will be a region of low surface atmospheric pressure. The equatorial belt is a region of generally low pressure.

At high altitude, the rising air cools, becomes more dense, and sinks. Where the sinking air reaches the surface the atmospheric pressure will be high. The edges of the tropics and the subtropics, where equatorial air is sinking, are regions of generally high pressure, one in each hemisphere. Although the air is very cold while it remains at a great height, as it sinks and is compressed it warms *adiabatically* (without mixing with surrounding air), so air in the tropical-subtropical regions is warm.

Over the poles, very cold air sinks to the surface. This produces generally high pressure.

Between the low-latitude high pressure and the high-latitude high pressure there is, in each hemisphere, a belt of generally low pressure.

Air movements carry warm air away from the tropics and cool air away from polar regions. This distributes the warmth we receive from the Sun more evenly than would be possible if the Earth had no atmosphere.

Although the Earth is heated most strongly in the tropics, all parts of the planet receive some warmth from the Sun, and land and water respond differently. Land warms and cools much faster than water. As air moves, it is warmed or cooled by the surface over which it travels.

Together, the transport of heat from low to high latitudes and the difference in the effect of heating on land and water generate the global circulation of the atmosphere. It is this circulation that produces regional climates and our day-to-day weather.

the intertropical convergence and its winds move south again and the winter pressure and wind systems return.

Further east, the summer monsoon affects all of southern Asia and extends eastward as far as southern Japan, although it is much less pronounced by then because the winds have lost much of their moisture over Burma, Thailand, and Vietnam. At Nagasaki (33°44' N) about 30% of the total annual rainfall occurs in June and July.

Summer and winter monsoons are caused by seasonal shifts in the distribution of pressure and winds, leading to a reversal in the direction of prevailing winds. In summer they blow one way and in winter from the opposite direction, bringing dry air from one direction and rain from the other. They are extreme in India and southern Asia, because of the size and height of the Tibetan Plateau and the huge area of the Asian continent, but seasonal shifts of this kind occur throughout the tropics.

In winter, the northeasterly winds blowing down from the Tibetan Plateau and bringing the dry monsoon to India continue across the Arabian Sea, blowing almost parallel to the coast of East Africa. They have gathered moisture, but because they blow parallel to the coast and not across it, they bring no rain. Further north, however, the Asian northeasterlies gather no moisture. They blow across the arid Arabian peninsula and narrow Red Sea. At Addis Ababa, Ethiopia, an average of 6.2 inches of rain fall in the six months from October to March. In spring, as the intertropical convergence moves north, the southeasterly trade winds affect regions to its south, but they bring only small amounts of rain. It is in summer that the Asian summer monsoon exerts a strong influence. Southwesterlies then prevail and although they blow from the South Atlantic right across the African continent, they bring a pronounced rainy season. Addis Ababa receives an average of 28.3 inches of rain in the six months from April to September, July and August being the wettest months. This is the African monsoon. It affects southern Arabia and most of the eastern side of Africa in both hemispheres, from Ethiopia to northern Mozambique and also a smaller region of West Africa, from Côte d'Ivoire to Nigeria.

A similar but less pronounced seasonal reversal of pressure and wind direction occurs over the Gulf region of the United States. The seasonal difference in rainfall is not great everywhere, but at Miami an average of 15.4 inches of rain fall between November and April, and 43.4 inches between May and October. This is the American monsoon.

Monsoons matter most where the difference between the dry and wet seasons is most extreme, because then farmers depend on the monsoon rains, and the whole of their farming year is geared to them. If they arrive late there are difficulties, if they are lighter than usual crop yields will be reduced, and if they fail so will the harvest. Excessive monsoon rains cause difficulties that are nearly as serious. Then rivers burst their banks and there is widespread flooding.

Unfortunately, the Asian monsoon, which is by far the most important, has always been somewhat unreliable. From 1876 to 1879, between 14 million and 18 million people are estimated to have died from starvation in India and China because of famines due to the failure of the monsoon rains. They failed again twice in the early 1970s. On this occasion more than one million people are believed to have died in India and Bangladesh. These are the major failures, but there are less serious ones as well, when the rains arrive, but are light. There were several such years in the last century, and 1918 was another. More recently, 1965 was a year of low monsoon rainfall.

For those of us who enjoy climates which spread rainfall fairly evenly through the year it is easy to forget the extent to which the seasonal rains matter when almost no rain falls during the remainder of the year. People adapt to such extremely seasonal climates, but adaptation works only when the seasons are reliable. When the rains fail there is drought, and when there is drought there is hunger and often starvation.

COPING WITH DROUGHT

Dry-weather farming

Plants consist mostly of water, by weight. As they grow, they absorb water into their newly formed cells and use water to transport nutrients and provide mechanical support (see page 51). Some plants have adapted to desert conditions by storing water in their tissues and releasing as little of it as possible. A few of these plants are edible, but in general they are not the ones that supply us with food. Our crop plants have been bred over thousands of years to produce high yields of nutritious food, and most of the breeding took place in parts of the world where the rainfall is reliable and ample for their needs. Today, if the climate does not supply enough water the usual remedy is to provide irrigation (see page 99).

There is an alternative, however. In the middle of the last century, when the railroads were expanding westward across the United States, farmers followed. The federal government gave railroad companies grants of land extending up to 20 miles on either side of the track. This left the companies with more land than they needed, so they sold it to settlers at about $4 an acre. The federal government, seeking to raise funds as well as encourage settlers, also sold land to settlers and they charged only $1.25 an acre, but the closer farms were to the railroad the easier and cheaper it was for produce to be taken to market and equipment and supplies to be obtained. Farmers preferred to be close to the railroad, and the companies warmly welcomed and encouraged them.

After a time, free land also became available. The Homestead Act of 1862 gave 160-acre plots to people who would settle, farm, and improve them for five years. After five years, the settlers owned the land.

Hundreds of thousands of people were attracted by the offer of free land and joined those who had bought their farms. They came

from the eastern United States or were recent immigrants from Europe. In 1874, for example, colonies of Mennonites, a European Christian sect in this case comprising people of German ancestry who moved to the United States from Russia, bought 60,000 acres in Kansas.

All these immigrants had learned their farming on land watered by abundant rains. When they settled on their new lands they tried the farming methods they knew, but soon found them unsuccessful. The climate on the western side of the Great Plains was too dry, and the crops failed. The railroad companies urged the government to help the settlers and in 1906 the Bureau of Dry Land Agriculture was established.

It recommended a type of fallow farming. The farm is divided into two equal parts. A crop is grown on one half, then the land is left for a year while the other half is cropped. While the fallow land is "resting" it is plowed and harrowed. This destroys weeds and plants growing from seed left in the soil by the previous crop ("volunteer" plants). It also opens up spaces in the soil, allowing water to penetrate more easily, and removing all the plants prevents the loss of water by transpiration. For a whole year the fallow land gathers the water that falls on it. Inevitably, much of the water is lost, but enough remains to increase significantly the rate of seed

Figure 32: *Fields being irrigated with water derived from a well and drawn by a buffalo-powered pumping system in Uttar Pradesh, India, 1977.* (UN photo 137519/J.P. Laffont)

germination and early growth for the crop that follows. In effect, each annual crop is able to use more than one year's water. In 1909 the Enlarged Homestead Act amended the original act by doubling to 320 acres the free plots made available in areas where the climate was dry, recognizing that only half of it could be cultivated in any one year and stipulating that settlers would be given permanent title to their land if they farmed 80 acres of their homestead for five years.

This type of agriculture is called "dry farming" and it proved highly successful throughout the drier regions of the American West. Farmers in the Palouse region, in southeast Washington state and extending into parts of Oregon and Idaho, still grow wheat and peas in this way, although they now grow a different crop in each field every year, rather than leaving land fallow. Like the prairie grasses native to the area, wheat can send its roots 6 feet deep in search of water. This sustains it through the dry summer months, and yields are high.

American farmers developed their own dry-farming methods by trial and error, but they are not unique, even in North America. While they were experimenting, the Hopi had already been dry farming for a very long time, in Arizona. They chose shallow depressions where water was most likely to collect, and cultivated them from April to July. Hopi farmers cleared the natural vegetation to make small fields and sowed each field with melons, squash, beans, and several different varieties of corn, and erected wind-breaks to reduce evaporation and soil erosion. Success depended on rain at just the right time during the growing period. That was always uncertain, but when the plants received the water they needed, crop yields were adequate.

Thousands of miles away, in Sudan, nomadic peoples also developed a very similar type of dry farming. There the average annual rainfall varies from a mere 5 to 8 inches and in some places is only 4 inches, so the land is desert. The rain all falls in three or four months, however, so it is concentrated. Like the Hopi, the Sudanese farmers cultivate shallow depressions and grow sorghum (*Sorghum vulgare*), a kind of millet that looks much like corn while it is growing and produces grain that is ground into flour resembling cornflour, but with a higher protein content. Versions of dry farming are also found in other parts of North Africa and in Southwest Asia. The method is obviously ancient. Southwest Asia, where wheat and barley were first domesticated, is one of the regions where farming began, so perhaps dry farming is the oldest of all types of agriculture.

Dry farming is very different than farming with no water at all. That would be impossible. It is farming in a dry climate on land with no irrigation. It amounts to using such water as there is in the most efficient way and reducing losses to a minimum.

In Israel there are orchards growing pomegranates in places where the annual rainfall averages 6 to 8 inches. The trees are very

widely spaced, making the orchard look more like a scattering of isolated shrubs than the orchards you find in Europe or America. Desert shrubs naturally grow far apart from one another. If they were closer together their competition for the available water would

Figure 33: *Irrigated fields in Kibbutz en Gedi, Israel.* (Israel Ministry of Tourism)

kill all of them. The Israeli orchards are designed the way they are for the same reason. Each shrub, slightly taller than a man, stands at the center of a small basin dug into the desert surface. Rain and dew flow down the sides of the basin and provide the shrub with enough moisture to survive.

There are other versions of this method. On a gentle slope, level fields can be made at intervals. When it rains, water flows down the slope and onto the field. A ridge at the farther end prevents the water running off the field. As drawing A in figure 34 shows, each field, made as a terrace, catches and holds all the water flowing down the slope. If the ground is level, slopes can be made, as in drawing B. In this case, there can be a series of sunken terraces each of which catches water flowing into it from either side.

Often the retention of water is helped by working a layer of dead plant material, usually the residue of a previous crop, into the surface soil. Barley has been grown successfully in this way in California, producing 93 pounds of grain for every acre-inch of rainfall (an acre-inch is the amount of rainfall that would cover one acre to a depth of one inch). The system seems to work most efficiently when a crop is grown in each sunken terrace every year, but sometimes terraces are left fallow in alternate years.

Plant material worked into the surface is called a *mulch* and gardeners often use it to suppress weeds and retain water. They also reduce evaporation by shading the soil, which keeps it cool. Mulches do not have to be made from vegetation, although this is a useful way of disposing of stubble, surplus straw, and other wastes. Gravel and a variety of other materials are also used. Spreading mulches is not such hard work as it sounds. There are machines that scoop up soil from the surface, sieve it to collect the gravel present naturally in it, then spread the gravel back on the surface as a mulch.

Conventional mulches slow the rate at which water evaporates from the soil, but they do not prevent evaporation altogether. If conditions remain dry for weeks on end, both mulch and soil will dry. Moisture can be retained much longer if the ground is covered by opaque plastic sheeting with holes punched in it, through which the crop plants are sown. Plastic sheeting is widely used in growing

Figure 34: *Conserving water.*

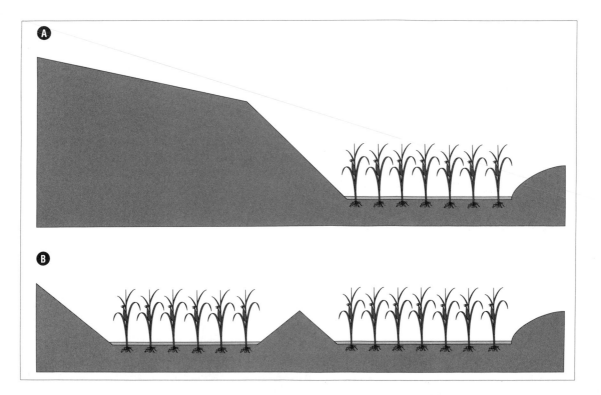

horticultural crops, even in areas of abundant rainfall, because it is often the cheapest and most effective way to control weeds without using herbicides. Plastic sheeting is even used to collect water. Where plants are grown in shallow depressions or sunken terraces, if the whole area is covered with sheeting, dew condensing on the plastic at night will trickle downhill to the plants and be absorbed by them before the morning Sun evaporates it.

It is impossible to grow crops if there is no water at all, but dry-farming methods make do with surprisingly little. They have been developed wherever in the world rainfall is sparse, and although they cannot produce yields as large as those from well-watered land, throughout history they have helped make dry regions habitable.

Irrigation

Mexico City lies 7,575 feet above sea level on a large plain surrounded by mountains. It receives about 30 inches of rain a year, 90% of it between May and October. From November to April the rainfall amounts to only 3 inches. The climate is healthy, but so dry in winter that crops can be grown only if water is brought to them. If you visit the city today you will find there are many canals. These are not for transport, however. They are what remains of one of the most remarkable agricultural systems the world has ever known.

When the first Europeans arrived in Mexico, in 1519, they found an empire ruled from the Aztec capital of Tenochtitlán-Tlatelolco, located where Mexico City is now. At that time, a large lake covered about one-quarter of the valley in summer. In winter, as water evaporated, this was reduced to five smaller lakes. One of these, Lake Xochimilco, to the south of the city, was fed by springs on its southern shore, where the water table was higher than the surface of the water in the lake. The ground there was swampy, and local farmers had drained the land by digging canals. This allowed clean, fresh water to flow more freely into the lake and from there into the deeper Lake Texcoco, to the north.

The canals were of various widths, but they ran more or less parallel to one another and were linked by other canals at right angles, making a grid pattern. Mud dug from the bottom of the canals was piled on the land between them, raising it higher and creating a system of narrow islands surrounded by canals and peninsulas into the lake. These islands and peninsulas were called *chinampas*. At first they were kept in place by branches and vines woven between posts around their edges. Later, many of these fences were replaced by willow trees.

Each *chinampa* is about 300 feet long and 15 to 30 feet wide, and the *chinampas* are cultivated. Farmers travel between them in flat-bottomed boats, which they also use when dredging mud from the beds of the canals. This keep the canals open and provides fertilizer for their plots. Water plants grow in the canals. These are gathered by the farmers and towed, like huge rafts, to be spread on the plots and then covered with mud to keep the plants moist while they compost. Carp and other fish are also raised in the canals. In modern times, the *chinamperos*, who cultivate the *chinampas*, say that each year they can raise two crops of corn and five of other plants from each plot.

The area around Xochimilco became part of the Aztec state in the 15th century and the high productivity of the *chinampas* probably helped sustain the Aztec Empire, but this farming system is much older. Scientists believe the first *chinampas* may have been dug about 2,000 years ago.

At first, it is likely that the *chinampas* were dug in order to drain the swamps. It was land reclamation, similar to that which has provided fertile farmland in the Netherlands and parts of eastern England, but it went much further because the canals also provided water for crops throughout the dry season as well as vegetation and mud, giving each *chinampa* its own compost heap. Water was removed from where it was not needed and delivered to where it was needed in a very efficient system of resource management.

Knowledge of the system may have spread north into what is now Arizona. *Hohokam* means "those who have gone" in the language of the present native Americans who live in the area around Salt River, but it refers to a people who are believed to have moved there from Mexico in around 300 B.C. They were farmers who cut a total of 150 miles of irrigation ditches, some of them 30 feet wide and 10 feet deep, and grew corn, beans, squash, and cotton. Their irrigated farming system supported a population large enough and with enough spare time to build towns and develop arts, trade, and government. Then, soon after A.D. 1400, the Hohokam people vanished and their canals were abandoned. No one knows why this happened, but it may be that their farming succumbed to the greatest danger facing any irrigation system and the fertility of their land was destroyed.

Where the climate is dry, the most obvious way to make farming possible is by directing such water as there is to the cultivated area. This is irrigation, and it has been practiced for thousands of years and discovered independently in many places. Today, 99% of all the water available in Egypt is used to irrigate crops. Egyptian farmers were irrigating their land 4,000 years ago and they probably learned how to do so from the farmers of the Fertile Crescent. This is the area between and to either side of the rivers Tigris and Euphrates, in modern Syria and Iraq. It is where civilization first developed. Farms and towns were starting to develop in the area 8,000 years ago, and within a short time those farms were being supplied with irrigation. You might say, therefore, that irrigation is as old as civilization itself.

Irrigation canals are often dug from the sides of rivers, to divert part of the flow around the edges of fields. Dams are often built to make artificial lakes from which water can be channeled into irrigation systems.

Where there is no suitable river, the simplest method involves digging a well to gain access to the groundwater and pouring water from the well into irrigation ditches. The traditional ways of doing this have been in constant use for thousands of years. Eight to 10 feet above the well, a horizontal beam supports a long, tapering, horizontal pole. A bucket is hung from the longer, thinner end and counterweights are fixed to the shorter, thicker end. A person pulls on a rope to make the bucket descend into the well. When it is full, the counterweights swing the pole to raise the bucket, and the person then tips the water into a channel feeding into the network of ditches. The device is called a *shaduf* in Egypt. In some parts of India it is called a *denkli* and in other parts a *paecottah*. It can irrigate about 2 acres.

Alternatively, draft animals (usually oxen) can be used to turn a vertical wheel. Buckets are attached to ropes passing over the wheel in such a way that while half the buckets are descending the other half are rising. When they reach the top the buckets tip automatically, pouring their water into channels.

Digging canals and pouring water onto the land from buckets requires little technological skill, but some traditional irrigation methods are much subtler. In parts of the Sahara, for example groundwater is used to increase the size of oases. Gently sloping channels have been built to collect groundwater and direct it to the oasis. The channels, called *foggaras*, were covered over after they had been made, so they run below ground.

Farmers in the Negev Desert, in Israel, invented a method to "harvest" water during the Israelite period, about 950–70 B.C. and extended it during the Nabatean and Roman-Byzantine periods, from about 300 B.C. to A.D. 630. Annual rainfall in the Negev is about 4 inches a year, but it falls as heavy local showers that send torrents racing down river channels and cause flash flooding.

The ancient farmers built low walls to capture this water and direct it to terraces of fields in a low-lying area. Water entered one field, was allowed to remain there long enough to soak the ground, then flowed over a spillway to the next field below, and so on until what remained drained into an underground storage tank. If this seems similar to modern methods of dry farming (see page 94) perhaps it is because the modern methods are based on those of the ancient Nabateans. This system made it possible to supply fields with five times more water than rain falling directly on them could deliver. At its height, it allowed some 500,000 acres of the Negev to be farmed, supporting thousands of farming families and six towns. Eventually, the channels fell into disuse and knowledge of the Nabatean farms was lost. It is only in recent times that archaeologists, working in what is now desert, have traced the lines of their walls and reconstructed the way the system worked. The terraces are now being restored by Israeli workers, who use concrete rather than desert stone to build the walls.

Water can be lifted by hauling on ropes to raise buckets or by turning a wheel, but there is another, altogether more ingenious method. It is called the *Archimedes screw*, suggesting it was invented in Syracuse, Sicily, by that city's most famous son, the Greek mathematician and engineer Archimedes (*c.* 287–*c.* 212 B.C.), although some people believe the Egyptians were using it long before Archimedes was born. As its name suggests, the screw is a cylinder, about 10–15 feet long, on the surface of which there is a spiral flange, like the thread on a screw. The device is tilted at an angle with the lower end in water. As it is turned, water is lifted up the "thread" and spills out from the top. Ancient though it is, the Archimedes screw is still used today, industrially as well as for lifting irrigation water.

On most modern farms, however, the most common irrigation device is the sprinkler. Water is pumped to it and sprayed through rotating nozzles. When the area it reaches has been thoroughly soaked, the sprinkler is moved. Some farm sprinklers are self-propelled, traveling slowly in a straight line under their own power. The farm sprinkler works the same way as the garden lawn sprinkler, but is bigger.

Unfortunately, irrigation can cause serious problems. Often, it is wasteful. Obviously, it is in hot, dry weather that crops need irrigation most, but that is also when the rate of evaporation is highest. Of the clouds of spray ejected from sprinkler systems, up to 30% of the water may evaporate without reaching the ground, although losses can be reduced by sprinkling at night, when lower temperatures mean less evaporation.

In many places, irrigation water is taken from the groundwater. This can remove water from an aquifer faster than the flow into it. When this happens, the water table falls, so wells and boreholes have to penetrate to a greater depth. Eventually, though, the water table may sink too deep to be reached. This is serious, but near sea coasts there is an even greater danger. If the water table falls below sea level, sea water will start flowing into the aquifer. The salty sea water is denser than the fresh water and pushes beneath it, like a wedge. This displaces the fresh water, but also mixes with it to some extent, so the water being used for irrigation becomes increasingly salty. Eventually, the salt concentration can be enough to poison crop plants.

Saltwater intrusion is a risk only near coasts, but salts can destroy land anywhere. *Salinization* is the accumulation of salt near the soil surface and it is closely linked to waterlogging. This is what may have destroyed the agricultural system developed by the Hohokam. The problem is both widespread and ancient.

Some of the water falling onto the ground as rain evaporates from the surface and the remainder drains away through the soil and eventually into rivers (see page 55). It flows constantly. Irrigation water may not flow. The aim is to wet the soil and to keep it wet, so there is a tendency to supply water faster than it can drain into the groundwater. This is usually highly successful. Crops grow well, yields increase, and farmers are happy. So they continue with the practice. Gradually, though, the water table is rising because the farmers are adding water faster than it is being removed. For a long time this may not be noticed. The water table is still well below the roots of the crop plants.

Then plant growth starts to falter. It may be that the water table has risen high enough to cover part of the root system. Roots need air for respiration. Some plants are more tolerant than others of having their roots submerged, but most crop plants soon start to suffer. Literally, some of their roots are drowning and are no longer able to absorb nutrients to sustain the plants. The soil is becoming waterlogged.

Waterlogging brings with it the risk of salinization. Irrigation water is never pure. It contains some dissolved mineral salts. If it flows away into the groundwater its salts are removed with it, but if the water table is rising they are not. Above the water table, water is drawn upward by capillarity and in the hot, dry conditions where irrigation is most useful, water evaporates from the surface. The water that evaporates is pure. At evaporation the water molecules detach from the dissolved salts, which are left behind in the soil, where they accumulate. Water moving upward dissolves them and the soil water becomes increasingly saline until it alters the balance between the solution inside root cells and the solution in the soil outside them. When the soil solution becomes more concentrated than the cell solution, pure water flows out of root cells instead of into them. This kills plants and by the time the crops fail the soil has become badly poisoned.

Remedying the situation is difficult. Salts can be removed from the soil by flushing it with fresh water, so the salts dissolve and are carried away. If the soil is waterlogged, however, this will not work unless the water table is lowered first. One method is to sink wells deep enough to penetrate well below the contaminated water (which has been applied from above and does not sink very far into the groundwater) and pump fresh water from there to the surface. This can be used to flush salts from the soil, and the amount that evaporates and is lost ensures that the water table continues to fall for as long as pumping continues.

This is costly and it is much better to foresee the danger and avoid it. If irrigation pipes are laid below the surface and deliver measured amounts of water directly to the soil around plant roots, evaporation will be minimized, the water table will not rise, and salinization will not occur. Many irrigation systems now work in this way.

Neither will soil become waterlogged or saline if drainage is installed at the same time as the irrigation system to ensure water used to irrigate crops flows out of the area, rather than accumulating. Probably by accident, this is the secret of the success of the *chinampas*. Because the springs supplying the irrigation water are higher than the water level in the lake at the other end of the canal network, water flows from the higher to the lower level. The irrigation water flows, and the plots it irrigates lie above the water level in the canals, so they never become waterlogged.

Irrigation makes it possible to grow crops in dry climates. This extends greatly the area of farmland available to feed us. In the world as a whole, there is at present more than 900 million square miles of irrigated farmland, and more than 60% of it is in regions with dry climates. About one-sixth of all cultivated land is irrigated and this land produces about one-third of the world's food. On average, the output from irrigated land is double that from land watered only by falling rain. Not surprisingly, the area of irrigated land has been increasing. Even where rainfall is moderate, irrigation can increase crop yields. It is an important technique and farmers have always known this. Unwise irrigation can poison the land, however, and this is something farmers have not always realized.

Water for people

Without water to drink, we die. If you minimize the loss of water from your body by resting in a cool place so you do not perspire, you are unlikely to survive longer than about a week if you have nothing at all to drink. In hot weather you may not live more than two or three days. Food is a less urgent requirement. You can survive several weeks without eating.

All the chemical reactions in our bodies take place in water. Of all the water in the body, about 60% is inside cells, 30% in body tissues between cells, and the remainder in the blood plasma. The total amount must be maintained in order to keep the concentration of dissolved substances constant. If the concentration changes, the osmotic pressure on either side of cell walls will also change, causing water to flow into or out of cells. If water flows out of cells they become dehydrated and eventually die. If water flows into them they swell. It is rare for people to drink so much water it makes them ill, but occasionally it happens and people have even died from water poisoning.

We need to drink at least 2.5 pints of water a day and more than that in hot weather or after any kind of physical exertion. Most people drink much more, not so much because they are thirsty as because they enjoy the taste of what they drink. Drink a cup of coffee or a glass of fruit juice and you do not think of it as water, but remove the flavoring, coloring, sugar, and a few other minor ingredients and that is what it is. When you are very thirsty you may eat fruit instead of drinking, but it is the water in the fruit that your thirst is demanding. Our food also contains water. Just as the human body is about 60% water by weight, so is most of the food we eat.

If your body loses more water than you drink to replace it, it will not be long before you feel ill. You may not feel thirsty. The first indication that you need more fluid may be a marked reduction in the amount of urine you pass. You may feel generally unwell and have trouble sleeping. Then your muscles will weaken. If your body weight falls by 2% due to dehydration the working capacity of your muscles may decrease by as much as 20%. For an adult man of average weight (140 pounds), this means losing about 5 pints of body fluid. If that man loses 7 pints he will be too weak to perform even the smallest tasks. His skin will feel dry and rather stiff and he may have hallucinations. If he loses between 14 and 18 pints he will die.

All animals need water, of course, but some are able to use it much more efficiently than humans. This enables them to survive in deserts, where they may find drinking water only occasionally. Some animals never drink at all, obtaining all the water they need from the food they eat. We are not like that. Our bodies lose fluid readily because we sweat to keep cool and maintain a constant body temperature. In hot weather, or when playing a strenuous sport, we can lose between 0.2 and 0.5 ounces of fluid an hour for every pound of body weight by sweating. A man weighing 140 pounds can lose 28–70 ounces of fluid per hour. We also lose water in our feces and urine, and when we breathe. Respiration involves the oxidation of carbon. This reaction releases energy, and the carbon dioxide and water we excrete when we breathe out are the byproducts.

Animals adapted to life in deserts can reduce even respiratory water loss and they produce very dry feces and very concentrated urine (see page 14). A human body, in contrast, loses an average of almost a pint of water a day in this way, as well as a similar amount in sweating and about one-quarter of a pint in feces. Even if you remain quite still and in a cool place, you cannot avoid losing about 2.5 pints of water a day because your kidneys need to use a certain minimum amount to remove the waste products from the ordinary chemical reactions that keep your body alive even when you are not eating. If you do not eat or drink to replace the fluid your body loses, it will take rather less than six days to lose 14 pints and just over seven days to lose 18 pints. This is how the length of time someone can survive without drinking is calculated.

Not surprisingly, people have always valued sources of clean, potable water. Natural springs and wells have often been associated with benign spirits and in some countries there are many "holy" wells associated with Christian saints. Usually there were rivers and sometimes lakes not far from such springs and wells, but these were less dependable. During droughts they dwindled and might even disappear, and their waters were not always pure. Drinking from them could cause illness.

Supplying enough water for everyone to drink safely is now a major challenge facing the world, mainly because of the cost of purifying it to a safe standard (see page 108), but partly because natural sources of fresh water are not distributed evenly throughout the world. In some regions, the amount of fresh water naturally

Figure 35: *Car wash in use, Philadelphia, Pennsylvania, 1996.* (1996, Christopher Speeth)

available per person per year is one-fiftieth of that available in others, and demand for fresh water is increasing rapidly in countries that are developing their manufacturing industries. In the world as a whole, we are now using almost four times more fresh water than we were using 50 years ago (254 cubic miles in 1945 and 990 cubic miles in 1995).

We do not drink more than a tiny fraction of all that water, of course. Indeed, the water that is piped into private homes accounts for only about 10% of it, and even then the amount we drink is insignificant. We drink at most a few pints of water a day, but when we take a bath the tub usually contains more than 30 gallons. Flushing the toilet uses 5 gallons, and if we leave the water running while we wash the dishes after a meal it is easy to use about 30 gallons. Depending on whether it is set to a full or economy load, a washing machine uses between about 20 and 45 gallons each time it is used. All of this water can be recycled, and whether it is recycled or not eventually it is returned to the sea. The total amount of water on the planet does not alter.

Much more water than this is used in factories. In North America and Europe four to five times more water is used by industry than is supplied to private homes. Some is incorporated into manufactured products, but most is used for cooling or as an ingredient in the manufacturing process. The textile, iron and steel, and petrochemical industries use large amounts of *process water*. Process and cooling water can be used again or cleaned and returned to the source from which it was taken, but a proportion is lost by evaporation each time it is heated. Factories in the United States use water an average of nine times before they finally discharge it, and by the end of the century they are expected to be using it 17 times.

Many of the great industrial cities of the world lie beside rivers or on the shores of lakes, close to a convenient source of the water they need. Obtaining this water may involve nothing more complicated than a channel to divert water into a factory or pumps to force it into the pipes that deliver it. Where water is taken from a deep lake, however, there is a chance to match the supply to the demand more precisely. In the Great Lakes, for example, vertical towers set on the lake bed have inlets at various depths. The temperature and chemical composition of lake water vary with depth and different inlets supply different requirements. If surface water is not available or the amount is insufficient, groundwater can be tapped (see page 55).

River water may be suitable for industrial use, but not fit to drink, in which case a source of clean drinking water must be found, and once obtained, the water must be moved to where it is needed, perhaps a distance of several miles. A channel to carry water is called an *aqueduct*. The earliest were underground pipes carrying water from a spring to a pool, but in Roman times magnificent overhead aqueducts were built to serve many towns in southern Europe. Aqua Marcia, built in 144 B.C., was almost 56 miles long, 5.9 miles of it supported on tall arches. Like all aqueducts, it carried water downhill from hilltop springs to people living at a lower level.

Rome lies on the Tiber River, the waters of which have never been drinkable. By A.D. 97, the water supply for the city was carried by nine aqueducts delivering a total of 38 million gallons a day inside the city walls and a further 20 million gallons for those living outside the city walls. The tradition continues: the modern Apulian aqueduct carries 132 million gallons of water a day from the western side of the Apennines, through a 9.5-mile tunnel, and then to the city of Taranto, 152 miles away in the dry southeastern corner of Italy.

Rivers that provide water also carry away wastes and byproducts. Provided the amounts are small, rivers are able to cleanse themselves. Pollution becomes serious when contaminants are discharged into them in amounts that exceed this self-cleansing capacity. Such pollution increases the difficulty and cost of providing safe drinking water.

Water recycling and purification

Drought makes water pollution worse and can lead to the pollution of waters that were previously clean. This increases the cost of making water safe to drink just when people wish to use more water because of the intensely dry weather.

The link between drought and pollution is simple. Substances that enter water mix with it. Usually within a short time they have been greatly diluted, especially if the water is flowing. How diluted they become depends on the volume of water with which they mix. During a drought, rivers carry less water, often very much less, and the water level falls in lakes and ponds. There is less water to dilute the contaminants and so their concentration increases. If the amount of a substance entering the water remains the same, but the volume of water receiving it is reduced by half, the concentration of the pollutant doubles. This could increase a level of contamination that is safe to a level that is not.

Even if the polluting substance is not poisonous to humans in itself, it may nevertheless lead to poisoning. Nitrates and phosphates, for example, are plant nutrients. Most reach water in water draining from adjacent land, but they are also contained in sewage. They can stimulate the growth of algae, which are simple aquatic plants, or cyanobacteria, even simpler organisms that grow in water. If the water is warm or hot, as it is likely to be during a drought, they will grow even faster. Some of these organisms produce poisons in amounts large enough to make people swimming in the water seriously ill or even to kill them.

Natural surface water is never pure. Rainwater is slightly acid because of the carbon dioxide, nitrogen oxides, and sulfur dioxide that dissolve into it from the air. It contains solid particles of soil, and of soot and dust from factories. Rivers carry silt particles and chemical compounds draining from the land on either side. Groundwater may be safe to drink but it usually contains dissolved minerals, and these can be present in harmful concentrations. Wells can be contaminated by other water draining into them and they often harbor disease-causing bacteria. Before it is piped to our homes, water must be purified. We drink only a small proportion of the water we use, of course, and from time to time people suggest separating the water supply so we have one tap of drinking water and another for other uses. Duplicating all the plumbing would be very expensive and such a dual system would lead to health risks. Might young children accidentally drink from the wrong tap? Drinking water should be used to wash and cook food, but which tap should we use to wash the dishes? Would it be safe to bathe or wash clothes in water that is not fit to drink?

Even with a dual system, the low-quality water would still require some purification to prevent the spread of disease. Bacteria found in polluted water include those that cause cholera, dysentry, typhoid fever, and paratyphoid fever. Hopefully, poliomyelitis will be eliminated entirely from the world within the next few years, but at one time the virus that causes it was probably spread partly through contaminated water.

In practice, all water is treated to make it safe to drink before it enters the domestic supply. Water for industry may not need to meet such a high standard, however. The quality a factory requires depends on how the water will be used.

Most factories recycle their water. American factories use water an average of nine times before they finally discharge it. Even then, of course, it must be cleaned of substances that might harm aquatic plants and animals. Water for domestic use can also be recycled. The treatment which purifies it once can purify it a second time. This happens where many communities take water and discharge waste water along the course of a long river. People in the Netherlands, for example, drink water from the Rhine. Before it reaches them it has also supplied many small towns as well as the cities of Basel in Switzerland; Strasbourg in France; and Karlsruhe, Ludwigshafen, Mannheim, Mainz, Koblenz, Bonn, Cologne, and Düsseldorf in Germany. By the time the Rhine discharges into the North Sea, its waters have been drunk countless times.

Treatment to purify water starts as soon as the water is taken from its source. It begins with screening. The water passes through a row of iron bars, about 4 inches apart, to remove bottles, tree branches, and other large objects. Then it is allowed to stand while grit and smaller particles settle to the bottom. Copper sulfate is often added to prevent the growth of algae. Once the water is more or less clear it is ready to be pumped to the treatment plant.

There it is filtered through activated carbon. This is charcoal that has been heated by steam or hot carbon dioxide to 1,650° F, which makes it very porous. Activated carbon is very good at absorbing chemicals that give water a bad taste or smell. After that, chlorine is added. Chlorine dissolves in water and is then a powerful oxidizing agent that kills bacteria. Ozone is also very effective and is used in some treatment plants. The water is then passed through very fine filters to remove most of the tiniest particles suspended in it. Even finer particles cannot be removed by straining the water through filters. They must be made to gather into bigger lumps which settle to the bottom. This process is called *coagulation* or *flocculation* and it involves adding a compound the molecules of which attract and hold the particles. Aluminum sulfate ("alum") is often used, but ferric sulfate, ferric chloride, and calcium hydroxide (lime) are also suitable.

The water is then filtered again, this time by passing it through a bed of sand, sometimes comprising several layers. It may flow down through the bed under its own weight, or be forced through under pressure in a closed vessel. Both produce the same effect, but filtration under pressure is quicker. After filtration, the water is aerated by bubbling air through it. This introduces oxygen, which will oxidize any organic material that still remains unoxidized, and it also improves the flavor of the water. Finally, more chlorine is added to disinfect the water, and after disinfection, potassium permanganate or sodium thiosulfate is added to remove any remaining chlorine. The water is then ready to enter the domestic supply.

At every stage of treatment, and especially near its completion, water samples are analyzed. Routine analysis measures the pH (acidity or alkalinity) and the hardness of the water (the concentration of magnesium, iron, and calcium salts, which affect the ease with which water forms a lather with soap), and detects the presence and concentration of a range of substances. These must not be present in amounts greater than certain specified limits.

The concentration of pollutants, and the maximum concentrations permitted, are often measured in parts per million (ppm), or in some cases parts per billion (ppb). It is difficult to understand what "one part per million" and "one part per billion" really mean. Suppose you had one teaspoonful of some substance you wanted to dilute to a concentration of one part per million. You would need to mix it thoroughly in 1,100 gallons of water. That is about enough water to fill a tank 5 ft square and 6 ft deep. One teaspoonful diluted to one part per billion would require enough water to fill a pool about 50 yards long, 33 yards wide, and 10 feet deep. That permitted limits are set in parts per million or parts per billion demonstrates the sensitivity of modern scientific instruments used for analysis and also the care that is taken to protect public health.

Accidents can and do happen, of course. Occasionally an unusual contaminant finds its way into water unnoticed, passes through the treatment process, and remains undetected. Treatment is not designed to neutralize or remove it, and no test is applied to look for it, because no one has any idea it is present until it makes someone ill.

It can also happen that a pollutant enters water and escapes into the supply before it can be stopped. That is what happened in July 1988 at Camelford, a small town in Cornwall, in the southwest of England. A load of 20 tons of aluminum sulfate intended for flocculation was delivered to an unmanned water treatment plant and should have been poured into a storage tank. The tanks were unmarked, however, and the driver, unfamiliar with the site, mistakenly poured the chemical into the tank from which water was about to be released into the supply. Water containing up to 4,000 times the permitted amount of aluminum was sent into the pipes serving 22,000 people. The water was very acid (pH 4.2). It curdled milk, stung the lips and mouths of people who tried to drink it, and reacted with lead, zinc, copper, and other metals in the pipes, adding to the contamination. To clean out the pipes, officials flushed them with clean water and poured everything into local rivers, killing between 43,000 and 61,000 salmon and trout as well as countless other fish. Fortunately, such incidents are rare.

Diseases are transmitted by bacteria and viruses present in sewage. All of these should be killed by chlorine during the treatment process because chlorine destroys the proteins present in bacterial cells walls and viral coatings. To make sure, there is a test that detects the presence of bacteria in water. Bacteria and viruses are present in organic matter, on which bacteria feed. These bacteria use oxygen, so if the water is polluted with organic matter, the amount of oxygen dissolved in it will decrease with time as the bacteria consume it. The test for *biological oxygen demand* (or BOD) measures the amount of dissolved oxygen, from which the presence of bacteria can be calculated, and where there are bacteria there are usually viruses. If the water has passed through treatment and still has an unacceptably high BOD, it must be passed through the purification processes again. The amount of oxygen in a one-liter (1.75-pint) sample is measured, the sample is stored for 5 days in darkness at a constant temperature of 20° C (68° F), and the amount of oxygen is measured again. The difference indicates the degree of bacterial activity. Clean river water should have a BOD of about 0.0025 milligrams per liter. The BOD of raw sewage is about 100,000 times greater than that. Oxygen used by the bacteria is taken from the oxygen dissolved in water. This is also the oxygen on which fish and other aquatic animals depend, so raw sewage kills them by asphyxiation and is very strongly polluting.

Waste water should be treated to remove most pollutants before it is discharged into rivers, lakes, or coastal waters. It is this treatment that removes sewage as well as industrial chemicals.

In most countries great care is taken to ensure that the public water supply is safe. Treatment is costly, however, and in poor countries where cities are rapidly expanding it is not available everywhere. Drought adds to the dangers by increasing the concentration of pollutants just when demand for water is at its highest.

Desalination

Earth is a watery planet. Water covers more than two-thirds of its surface, and this vast store of water is inexhaustible. No matter how it is used, all water eventually returns to the store. Some evaporates and falls as rain. Rivers return the rest. It is recycled constantly. If you were an alien approaching the solar system from your distant world, the first thing to strike you about our planet would be its abundant supply of water. If your advance party of explorers then returned to your ship and told you that the beings living in some parts of this world were desperately short of water you would find it very hard to believe. It would seem utterly impossible.

Closer examination would soon reveal the reason. Although Earth has so much water, almost all of it is poisonous to plants and animals living on dry land. They have to manage with the 3% of the total that is not poisonous and even then more than half of that 3% is frozen, in polar ice caps and glaciers, and some is in aquifers too deep to be reached. The planet may be wet, but water remains a scarce commodity.

You might still find the situation puzzling because its solution is so obvious. The poisonous water contains dissolved salts, mainly sodium chloride (common salt) at an average concentration of about 3.5% (3.5 parts of salt to 100 parts of water). This is stronger than the solutions inside cells, so if cells are bathed in it water flows out of them by osmosis. Salt water thereby dehydrates cells, which can be fatal. The remedy is to remove the dissolved salts. Purify the water and it will no longer be poisonous. Then there will be more than enough water for every conceivable need.

Separating water from the salts dissolved in it is not difficult. It is called *desalination* (or *desalinization*) and there are many ways to do it.

Supply the water molecules with enough energy to break the hydrogen bonds linking them and they will escape from the liquid, leaving all the dissolved molecules behind. This is evaporation, of course, and it is how fresh water is made naturally.

Or you could do the opposite. Take energy away from the water until enough new hydrogen bonds have formed to change it into ice, a solid. Again, the process expels molecules other than those of water. This is freezing, and it is why icebergs are made from fresh water. In this case, desalination already occurs naturally on a large scale. All you need to do is attach cables to a suitable iceberg and tow it to where it is needed. It would melt as it entered warmer regions, of course, but there would still be plenty of it left by the time it reached, say, the deserts of the Middle East, and icebergs could provide a great deal of water. A big one may comprise several cubic miles of ice.

Then again, it is possible to make osmosis work in reverse. Ordinarily, when two solutions of different concentrations are separated by a semipermeable membrane with pores that allow water molecules to pass but not molecules of the dissolved substance, a pressure is exerted on the membrane that pushes water from the weaker to the stronger solution. Apply enough pressure on the other side of the membrane, however, and water will flow from the stronger to the weaker solution. If the weaker solution is pure water, reverse osmosis will add to it water removed from the salt water on the other side of the membrane.

Or electrodialysis can be used. Pour salt water into a vessel containing two electrodes. When a current flows through the water from one electrode to the other, the sodium and chlorine of the salt separate. The sodium ions have a positive charge and the chlorine ions a negative charge. Place a set of semipermeable membranes in the vessel, half of which allow positively charged ions to pass and half of which allow negatively charged ions to pass, and the sodium will move towards the negative electrode (the cathode), the chlorine towards the positive electrode (the anode), and pure water will be left in the middle of the vessel.

Sitting in your starship, somewhere out near Pluto, you may well be scratching your head (if you have one). Water shortage on Earth is a mystery. All of these methods work, and many more are technically feasible, but you have failed to spot two problems common to all of them.

The first is that they are expensive. In order to evaporate water you must heat it. That uses energy, for which you must pay. Freezing also uses energy, and if you plan to tow icebergs thousands of miles you will need ship with powerful engines that burn fuel. Reverse osmosis is an excellent technique, but to make it work you must increase the pressure on the semipermeable membrane to 25 times the surface atmospheric pressure. This takes a great deal of energy, and the electric current for electrodialysis has to be generated in some way. All the methods work, but all of them produce water that costs much more than water you simply take from a river, lake, or borehole. At present, in the United States, desalination plants can produce fresh water for $1 or more per 1,000 gallons, compared with the 30 cents it costs to supply clean water from a river, lake, or borehole.

Suppose people are prepared to pay for this expensive water. You can produce it, but now you face the other problem. What can you do with the residue that remains when you have separated the water from the salt? This will be a very strong brine. It is very poisonous and corrodes most metals. You cannot just pour it back into the sea. You could process it further to obtain the salts. For every thousand tons of fresh water, you would be left with 35 tons of salts. Unfortunately, there is no shortage of these and you would find it difficult to sell them for what it cost you to obtain them.

Despite the difficulties, however, fresh water is produced by the desalination of seawater in many countries. It is widely used in Israel, Kuwait, and Saudi Arabia, for example, as well as in Arizona, at the Yuma Desalting Plant, and at coastal towns in California. Key West, Florida, became the first U.S. city to obtain water by desalination when its multistage flash evaporation plant opened in 1967. United States research into desalination technologies is directed by the Bureau of Reclamation of the Department of the Interior. The cost has been reduced in various ways and is expected to reach 20–30 cents per 1,000 gallons. The concentrated brine can be stored and then diluted to make it suitable for release.

Reverse osmosis often produces fresh water more cheaply than other methods, but its rivals have been available for longer and are well established. Multistage flash evaporation is probably the most popular. Seawater is heated under pressure, which prevents it from boiling. It is then fed into a series of chambers, each at a slightly lower pressure. As it enters, some of the seawater boils instantly (it "flashes") and the remainder passes to the next chamber where more of it flashes. The vapor condenses as fresh water on pipes that pass through all the chambers for collection and removal. The pipes carry the incoming seawater toward the start of the process. Latent heat released by the condensation of the vapor warms the pipes, so the incoming water is fairly warm by the time it has to be heated. This saves fuel.

Vacuum freezing also exploits latent heat. In this process, seawater is cooled almost to its freezing point and then fed into a chamber where the pressure is very low. Some of the water vaporizes instantly, taking latent heat from the water around it. This lowers the temperature of the water, and some of it freezes. The ice crystals are separated from the brine and washed in fresh water, and then the pressure in the chamber is increased. This makes the vapor condense onto the ice crystals, releasing latent heat that melts the ice. The condensed vapor and melted ice are piped away as fresh water.

Dry regions often have hot climates, so there should be a way of obtaining the energy from the Sun to separate salt and water. One way has been found. It was invented by Lucien Bronicki, an Israeli engineer, and it uses a "salt-gradient solar pond" to generate electricity.

As its name suggests, the center of the desalination plant is a very large pond. The first one to be built, near Ein Bokek, Israel, has a surface area of nearly 8,000 square yards. At the bottom of the pond there is a layer of very salty water and at the surface a layer of almost fresh water. Sandwiched between these layers is a third layer of intermediately saline water. The Sun shines on the pond, its heat penetrating the upper layers and raising the temperature of the bottom layer. Although heated to 212° F or more, it cannot rise by convection because its high salt content makes it much denser than the water above it, as fresh water evaporates from the surface of the pond, more is added to replace it. Very hot brine from the bottom of the pond is then piped through a chamber containing a fluid with a low boiling point. This fluid vaporizes, expands, and is fed under pressure past a turbine. The spinning turbine drives a generator, producing electricity, and the vapor enters a second tank, where it is cooled by pipes carrying water from and back to the surface of the pond. The vapor condenses and is fed back into the first tank to be vaporized again.

If the electricity is used to separate salt from fresh water, some of the salt produced can be used to replenish losses from the bottom of the pond. There are many sites suitable for salt-gradient solar ponds in most dry-climate countries. There is one in Texas, built by the Army Corps of Engineers, although the power it produces is used to pump brine into a storage lake, preventing it from flowing into the Red River, rather than for desalination.

Not far from the coast in many desert countries there are shallow lakes or marshes lying at or just below sea level. Water evaporates rapidly from them and in many cases they are dry for at least part of the year. If sea water were pumped into them and then left to stand, evaporation would concentrate the salt to produce the dense bottom layer for a salt-gradient solar pond, onto which less salty water could be poured. This technology could supply very large amounts of fresh water fairly cheaply.

For most of our history, removing the salt to make sea water drinkable was not practical on a scale large enough to provide useful amounts of water. People had to make do with the fresh water that fell as rain, and if they lived in a dry climate they learned to value water highly and use it sparingly. Now that is changing. Already desalination is supplying affordable drinking water to coastal communities in many countries. In years to come it may satisfy the needs of many more, and visiting aliens will no longer be puzzled at a scarcity of water on such a watery planet.

Water storage

Long ago, almost at the dawn of history, the people living close to the Tigris River constructed a huge dam of earth to control the flow of the river. A little later another was built across the Nile, this time from rock. The Romans built many dams in North Africa and Italy, and dams were also built in India and Sri Lanka. For people living in a climate with a dry season, during which little or no rain falls, or where the rainfall is always unreliable, building a dam is an obvious way to store water. In other places, heavy seasonal rains or the melting of snow near the source of a river can cause sudden floods that destroy crops and wash away homes. Again, a dam can hold back the floodwaters and release them a little at a time so there is no flooding.

People have always built dams and they build them still. Only archaeological traces remain of the most ancient dams, but in 1995 there were more than 60,000 still in use and this figure counts only the larger examples more than 50 feet high. Together, these dams hold back about 1,500 cubic miles of water, and about 300 new dams are completed every year.

Technically, a "large" dam is defined as one that is more than 492 feet high, or holds back more than 19.6 million cubic yards of water, or forms a reservoir capable of containing 12 million acre-feet of water (enough water to cover 12 million acres to a depth of one foot). Some of those being built now are very large indeed. When it is completed, the highest in the world will be the Rogun Dam, on the Vakhsh River, Tajikistan. It will measure 1,099 feet from base to top. The distance along the crest of the Yacyretá-Apipe Dam, on the Paraná River near the border between Argentina and Paraguay, will be a little more than 43 miles. That dam is due to be completed in 1998. New dams are also being constructed in the United States. In California, the Seven Oaks Dam on the Santa Ana River, due to be completed in 1999, will be nearly 900 yards long, and Los Angeles and San Diego will eventually receive their water from the reservoir behind the Domenigoni Valley Dam. It will be able to store 1,321 million cubic yards of water, equal to 818,000 acre-feet.

This is big, but it is small compared with the real giants. Lake Oahe, behind the Oahe Dam in South Dakota, holds 23,600,000 acre-feet and Lake Mead, behind the Hoover Dam in Nevada, holds 31,047,000 acre-feet. Even this seems small beside the Volgograd

Dam on the Volga River, in Russia. Its lake holds 47,020,00 acre-feet, and the lake behind the Kariba Dam, on the Zambesi River between Zambia and Zimbabwe, holds 130,000,000 acre-feet.

Historically, most dams have been built to make artificial lakes to store water, but today many double as hydroelectric power plants. Some water flows continually from the reservoir and past turbines inside the dam itself, generating electricity and then entering the river downstream of the dam. The power output of such schemes can be very large. The Manwan Dam, for example, on the Lancang River (also called the Mekong) in China, generates 1.5 GW of power (1 gigawatt [GW] = one billion [10^9] watts), an output comparable to the largest of modern nuclear plants.

The earliest dams were made from earth, a material available in large quantities that is also easy to move because it can be carried in small loads. A valley would be sealed at the downstream end to make it fill with water. Many must have failed, sending huge volumes of water cascading into the lower ground downstream. Earth is still used and, although failure is still a risk with any dam, modern earth dams are safer than those built in the distant past because engineers have learned a number of rules that must be observed if the dam is to succeed.

If water flows through or beneath the dam it will wash away enough material to make the entire structure collapse, so the dam must be watertight. If the earth cannot be packed tightly enough to achieve this, a modern earth dam has a foundation and core made from an impervious material.

Water must not flow over the top of the dam. That too will wash away material and destroy the structure. Achieving this means studying the behavior of the river over several years. It is essential to know how much water the river carries at different times of year and the greatest volume of flow likely to be experienced. Then the dam can be built high enough to prevent waves ever washing over it, with a margin for safety between the top of the dam and the highest level the water is predicted to reach. This distance, between the highest water level and the top of the dam, is called the *freeboard*. Further protection is provided by making spillways to one or both sides of the dam. These allow surplus water to escape rather than overflowing the dam.

The shape of the dam is also important. As figure 36 suggests, the walls should have a shallow slope. On the upstream side this spreads the force of the water over a larger surface area, which protects the structure from being battered until it fails. This strengthening is often increased by covering the surface with a layer of large, loose rocks, called *riprap*. On the downstream side, the surface must be protected from rain. In time this can wash away enough material to cause failure. The surface can be protected by growing grass or

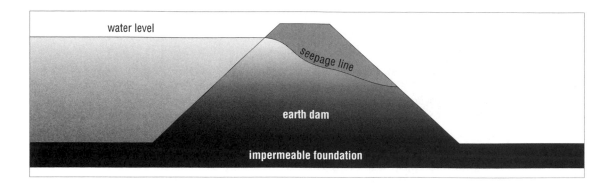

Figure 36: *Simple earth dam.*

other plants on it, and they are most easily planted and managed if the slope is not too steep.

In time, the pressure of water on the upstream side will cause the earth of the dam to become saturated. Water will then begin to flow through the dam below a *seepage line*. Unless the rate of seepage is controlled, eventually the dam will be weakened and will fail in a mudslide. Similarly, if the water level on the upstream side falls suddenly, water may not have time to drain from the saturated earth. Instead it will flow out rapidly, carrying earth with it, and cause a mudslide on that side. Again, the shallow slope helps by reducing the risk of material slumping to the bottom. Some dams also have a drain made from a layer of sand and gravel set into the impervious foundation beneath the dam near the downstream face. Seeping water is removed by the drain and the effect is to draw the seepage line back into the center of the dam, away from the downstream surface.

As dam construction developed, many earth dams came to be partly, and eventually completely, filled with rock and sealed by an outer skin of masonry. Other techniques were introduced and today there are many different ways to construct a dam. Engineers choose the one best suited to the site or design a dam incorporating elements from two or more basic types.

Damming a river is the most obvious way to make a large reservoir, but there is an alternative. Part of the river can be diverted along channels or pipes and taken into storage. The store can be outside the river valley through which the water was flowing before it was diverted, in a natural hollow or one excavated for the purpose.

At first, reservoirs were made to supply drinking water for humans and livestock. That is why the village ponds of Europe were dug. The provision of a reliable water supply to factories and homes is still important, but today most fresh water is used to irrigate farm crops, and on some rivers reservoirs are used to hold excess water that would otherwise cause flooding. Reservoirs suffer from two serious drawbacks. They lose a substantial amount of water by evaporation from their huge surface especially in low latitudes. This can amount to several feet of water a year and, of course, the rate of loss is greatest during drought, when the air is dry and hot. Over much of Australia, the potential evaporation rate is greater than, and in some places double, the annual rainfall. At Broken Hill, the average annual rainfall is 7 inches and the potential evaporation is 96 inches. Evaporation is reduced in some reservoirs by pouring enough oil onto the water to form a continuous layer one molecule thick over the entire surface, sealing the water from the air.

Sedimentation is the other problem. It shortens the life of all reservoirs and some are built larger than would otherwise be necessary simply to allow for sedimentation.

All rivers carry soil particles of various sizes suspended in their water. The amount the river carries depends on its energy, which is determined by its rate of flow. A dam brings the water to a standstill. As it loses energy the water also loses its capacity to carry silt and, small though they are, the particles sink to the bottom. There they accumulate as a layer of sediment that grows steadily thicker, raising the bottom of the reservoir and reducing the amount of water it can store. The sediment could be removed by dredging, but this is usually too expensive and we have to accept that the capacity of any reservoir will decrease gradually until eventually it is too shallow to be much use.

A reservoir is a lake, but it is not a natural one. It has been made by filling a natural hollow or valley with water. It occupies what was formerly dry land and most dry land is inhabited. For this reason, the construction of dams and their associated reservoirs often causes serious social disruption. The New China Dam in the Three Gorges region of the Chang Jiang (Yangtze) River in China is due for final completion in 2009. When completed, the dam will be about 1.2 miles long and the reservoir behind it will be 1,200 yards wide and 370 miles long. It is meant to prevent the floods that have occurred throughout history killing untold numbers of people, provide water where none was available previously, increase the size of the local fishing industry, and allow the expansion of industries that will provide much-needed employment. The valley is home to 750,000 people, however, and they will have to be relocated, most of them against their will. This is an extreme case, but most large reservoir projects cause similar problems and even if the site of the reservoir is not occupied by humans, it may include areas of great importance to wildlife conservation.

Planners will not proceed unless they are convinced that the benefits of a reservoir will exceed the disturbance its construction causes. The benefits are great and shared among the whole population of the region, but the people forced to abandon their homes and farms may bear an unfair proportion of the cost. Water is essential, but there are no simple answers to the problems associated with supplying it.

Saving water

Most reservoirs provide a range of recreational facilities. Visitors can walk around them, picnic on their shores, and use the water itself for sailing and fishing. They become popular attractions. When a new reservoir is proposed, however, there is usually strong resistance to the scheme. People do not like to see familiar valleys flooded, and the construction itself causes considerable annoyance to people living in the area.

The immediate response is to suggest that everyone economize. It is suggested that with a little care, we could manage perfectly well with the amount of water already available. More reservoirs are not really needed.

While this is an overstatement, and new reservoirs certainly are needed in some places, conserving water makes good sense. When you take a bath, for example, you probably use more than 30 gallons of water. Take a shower instead and you use much less water. With a regular shower head, you will use about 5 gallons of water a minute. Of course, if your shower lasts 7 minutes it uses more water than a bath in which you can soak for as long as you wish, but it is possible to halve the amount of water a shower uses by fitting an economy head. Then you will really save water. If there are 4 people in a household and they take one bath a day each, in a week they will use a total of 840 gallons of water. If, instead, they take a five-minute shower using an economy shower head, they will use 280 gallons a week. This is a considerable saving, and if the water supply is metered so you pay for the water you use, it also saves money.

Leaking taps also waste water. The amount seems small, but if a tap leaks one drop per second, in the course of a year it will drip 2,500 gallons.

A conventional toilet uses 5 gallons of water each time it is flushed. Again, savings are possible. A low-flow toilet uses less than 2 gallons. A family of four flushes the toilet an average of 20 times a day, so with a conventional toilet they use about 700 gallons of water a week. With a low-flow toilet this amount falls to about 225 gallons.

Garden watering uses even larger amounts of water. Family households use an average of 100 gallons a day to water the garden. This demand can be reduced by collecting rain water for garden watering, but during a drought the supply is soon exhausted. Some people use bath water to water the garden. This also helps. With some ingenious plumbing, bath water or water that has washed the dishes could be used to flush the toilet.

The amount of water used varies from place to place. In New York City, each person uses about 220 gallons a day for all domestic purposes, the people of Phoenix each use about 260 gallons a day, but in Tucson they use only 160 gallons. The demand in Tucson is lower than in other cities because its citizens were actively encouraged to save water by a range of measures, including the growing of native desert plants, which do not need watering, instead of lawn grasses, which do.

Over the United States as a whole, between 1950 and 1980 the amount of water used for all purposes increased from 1,200 to more than 2,000 gallons per day per person. Clearly, we could make do with less water and still have ample for drinking, preparing food, and cooking. These require no more than about 2 gallons a day for each person. Water can be recycled, of course. After it has been used, it can be collected, purified, and returned to the supply (see page 108). Even if the water is not considered safe for drinking, it can be made suitable for industrial use or crop irrigation.

There is a big disparity between the 2,000 gallons a day required for all purposes and the 250 or so used domestically. Most of this difference is accounted for by crop irrigation. Farms use about 80% of all the fresh water supplied in the United States, nearly all of it in the west, where water is most scarce. That is why many western cities now find themselves competing with farmers for water.

Industry uses about 8% of the fresh water supply. It takes about 400 gallons of water to extract and refine 1 gallon of gasoline and more than 50,000 gallons to make the automobile that burns it. Even making one soft drink cans uses about one-third of a pint of water when the amount needed for mining and refining the metal are included, although almost all of this water is used for cooling and washing, so it can be recycled many times.

Despite its economical use, water is still being extracted in Tucson several times faster than the sources of that water are being recharged. The problem has been eased, but not solved. Using less water is not merely a good idea. It is essential. Unless we learn to irrigate crops more efficiently, increase the number of times industrial water is recycled, and use less at home, eventually shortages will become acute and water rationing, for at least part of most years, will be inevitable.

Will climate change bring more droughts or fewer?

Climates are changing constantly and at various times in the past they have been very different from those we experience today. At one time, much of the land north of about 50° latitude was covered by a thick ice sheet. In medieval times northern Europe and America were warmer than they are today. Then after 1300 they cooled during the Little Ice Age, and did not start to warm again until the 18th century. Today scientists believe the average temperature over the whole world is rising. Over about the last century it is believed to have increased by about 1.8° F.

It has not been a steady warming. Temperatures fell from about 1940 until around 1980, although the total amount by which they fell is smaller than the amount by which they rose before 1940 and since 1980, so this century is warmer than the 18th and 19th centuries. The warming is not spread evenly. Arctic regions, north of 70° latitude, were colder from 1960 to 1986 than they had been between 1931 and 1960.

Most climatologists believe there is a link between average temperatures and the atmospheric concentration of certain gases and particles. Incoming solar radiation is predominantly shortwave (see box). The atmosphere is transparent to shortwave radiation, which passes through it like light through a window. It warms the surface, which then radiates back into space. The radiation from the surface is at long wavelengths. Air is not completely transparent to longwave radiation. Molecules of certain gases absorb it. They then radiate it but in all directions, and some of the radiation warms other gas molecules. This warms the atmosphere. It is rather like a greenhouse, which allows (shortwave) light to enter, but prevents (long-wave) heat from leaving, so the air inside the greenhouse is warmer than the air outside.

It is often called the "greenhouse effect," but is more properly known as the *enhanced greenhouse effect*. This is because the gases,

The solar spectrum

Light, radiant heat, gamma rays, X rays, and radio waves are all forms of electromagnetic radiation. This radiation travels at the speed of light as waves. The various forms differ in their wavelengths, which is the distance between one wave crest and the next. The shorter the wavelength, the more energy the radiation has. A range of wavelengths is called a *spectrum*. The Sun emits electromagnetic radiation at all wavelengths, so its spectrum is wide.

Gamma rays are the most energetic form of radiation, with wavelengths of 10^{-10}–10^{-14} μm (a micron, μm, is one-millionth of a meter, or about 0.00004 inch; 10^{-10} is 0.00000000001). Next come X rays, with wavelengths of 10^{-5}–10^{-3} μm. The Sun emits gamma and X radiation, but all of it is absorbed high in the Earth's atmosphere and none reaches the surface. Ultraviolet (UV) radiation is at wavelengths of 0.004–4 μm; the shorter wavelengths, below 0.2 μm, are absorbed in the atmosphere but longer wavelengths reach the surface.

Visible light has wavelengths of 0.4–0.7 μm, infrared radiation 0.8μm–1 mm, microwaves 1 mm–30 cm, then radio waves with wavelengths up to 100 km (62.5 miles).

especially carbon dioxide but also methane, nitrous oxide, and ozone, are present naturally in the air and they, together with water vapor, exert a natural warming, or greenhouse, effect. The present concern is that the burning of coal, oil, and gas, the clearing of forests, and certain farming practices add to the concentration of these "greenhouse" gases. Our activities may therefore enhance the natural greenhouse effect. CFCs (chlorofluorocarbons) also have a warming effect. Some particles also absorb long-wave radiation and warm the air. Others, especially of sulfur dioxide, reflect incoming shortwave radiation, which has a cooling effect.

If the concentration of these greenhouse gases were to double, making an allowance for the cooling effect of particles, scientists have calculated average temperatures would rise between 2.7° F and 8.1° F above their 1990 level, with a "best estimate" of 4.5° F. If we continue to add greenhouse gases to the atmosphere that doubling may occur around the year 2100.

A general warming over the entire world would shift the present climate belts. The equatorial and tropical belts would expand and the temperate regions would be pushed into higher latitudes. Tundra and polar climates would cover a smaller area. The reality is much more complicated. Warmer air would mean an increase in the evaporation of water. That would cool the water surface by removing from it the latent heat of evaporation, but water vapor is a powerful greenhouse gas and would have a warming effect. More clouds would form. This would also have a warming effect because of the release of latent heat as the vapor condensed. At the same time, precipitation would increase, and the clouds themselves might cool the air by reflecting incoming sunlight. Different regions would experience different kinds of change.

Calculating the effects of warming is very difficult, but it seems likely that air temperatures would increase more over land than over the oceans. Precipitation would increase in high latitudes and in the areas affected by the Asian monsoons (see page 86). Winter precipitation would increase the middle latitudes, but summers would be drier in some parts of the continents.

There would be very little warming in very high latitudes. With increased precipitation falling there as snow, the ice sheets might thicken rather than melting as some people have feared. Sea levels are already rising, partly because the oceans are expanding as they warm, but a thickening of the ice sheets would prevent them rising very far.

It appears, therefore, that a general warming of climates could increase the frequency and severity of droughts in the interior of continents. Elsewhere droughts are expected to become less common.

These predictions are much less certain than they may seem. So far there is no conclusive evidence of climatic warming that can be attributed to heat absorption by greenhouse gases, although mathematical models of the world climate that take account of all the factors believed to be influencing it correspond with the changes that have been observed. These models suggest that the combination of warming due to the enhanced greenhouse effect and cooling due to airborne particles are enough to explain the changes. This is not evidence that "enhanced greenhouse warming" has been detected, only that it is plausible. There might be another explanation, and despite the care with which they have been made, the measurements on which the observed changes are based might be inaccurate. It is extremely difficult to measure temperature changes with accuracies to fractions of a degree and to compare these with long-term averages. The measurements must allow a margin for error, and if the temperature rise is genuine it could be part of a natural variation operating over decades.

The influence of the oceans in transporting heat away from the equator is not completely understood, and neither is the fate of some 20% of the carbon dioxide being released into the air. It neither accumulates in the air nor dissolves in the oceans. No one knows what happens to it, although some of it is probably absorbed by plants, making them grow faster.

Nevertheless, there are other indications of warming. Since about 1950, average wind speeds and the number of wind storms have been increasing. This is probably, but not absolutely certainly, linked to a rise in tropical sea-surface temperatures of about 0.5° F since 1960 because warm tropical seas favor the formation of tropical cyclones (hurricanes, typhoons, and cyclones). Rainfall over the sea also seems to have increased. So, presumably, has the overall amount of water vapor in the atmosphere, due to increased evaporation. These indications may have nothing whatever to do with our release of greenhouse gases.

There are other uncertainties. From the 1940s to 1970s carbon dioxide was accumulating in the atmosphere faster than at any time before or since, yet temperatures were falling. Perhaps the fall was due to the even faster accumulation of atmospheric particles from factories that had not then installed equipment to reduce the pollution they caused, but no one can be sure. Nor can we realistically compare changes being observed now with changes that took place in the past, because we do not have enough reliable records. It is known, however, not only that climate does change, but that the amount by which it changes also varies.

There is a reliable record of one warm period. During the 1530s, the summers were as warm or warmer than those of the warmest years of our own century and the weather was also dry. People might well have thought the climate was growing steadily warmer. From 1536 to 1539 the English harvests were so good grain prices fell, and in 1540 there was drought from February until the middle of September. Cherries ripened by the end of May and the cereal harvest was early as well as abundant, although cattle died from thirst when streams and wells ran dry. Then the weather changed. Early in 1541 a hard winter began and, 20 years later the winter of 1564–65 was the harshest for centuries. In London, people played football on the frozen Thames. That severe winter heralded the onset of the coldest part of the Little Ice Age.

Doubts are justified, but they do not provide grounds for complacency. Climate change and the enhanced greenhouse effect are the subjects of intense scientific research and although much remains to be learned, so far the results support the idea that by releasing greenhouse gases we may trigger a general climatic warning.

Clearly we should take the calculations seriously and if there are ways to reduce the amounts of gases we release into the air we should pursue them. If we really are changing the climates of the world it would be very unwise to continue doing so, because the outcome might be highly disruptive. At least in some areas, droughts could become more frequent.

Index

Italic numbers indicate illustrations.

A

ablation 27
absolute vorticity 48, 49
acacias 18, 20
accidental drought *see* contingent drought
Addis Ababa 71
    rainfall in 93
adiabatic cooling 5, 12, 28
adiabatic warming 6, 11, 12, 92
Africa 1, 3, 16, 17, 18, 20, 34, 40, 47, 93
    deaths from drought 85
    East 70, 84, 93, 93
    North 69, 96, 116
        definition of drought in 64
    southern 42
    West 39, 84, 85, 89, 93
air, circulation of 5, 6, 7, 8–9, *22*, 22, 23, 31, 36, 43, 82, 90, 91–92
three-cell model 8, 9, 23, 31
air currents 5
    vertical 29
air density 6, 12, 92
air molecules 72, 122
air pressure 37, 38, 39, 43, 45, 92
Asian 90
    distribution of *43*, 90, 92
    and polar front 48
    surface 45–46, 45
air temperature 5, 6, 11, 12, 123
    and water content 10–11

variation with height 6, 12
Akkad 66–67, 68
Alaska 3, 35
Alberta 3
algae 108, 110
Algeria 11
aluminum sulfate 110, 111
ammonia 25, 26
Anchorage 3
Andes 37
Angola 84
angular momentum 48
    conservation of 48
angular velocity 48
Antarctica 20–24, 34
    dry valleys in 20, 21, 24
    precipitation 21–22
Antarctic Circle 34, 91
anticyclone 49–50
    blocking 50, 86, 87
anticyclonic flow 49
Antilles Current 31
Apennines 108
Aqua Marcia 108
aqueduct 107–108
Appulian 108
aquifer 61–62, 71, 72, 102, 112
    confined 62, 63–64
    perched 64
    recharge 65, 71, 85
    sea water contamination 102–103
    unconfined 62–63, 64
Arabian Desert 6, 20
Arabian Sea 91, 93
Archimedes 102
Archimedes screw 102

Arctic air 50
Arctic Circle 47, 79, 91
Arctic Ocean 34
Argentina 116
aridity, calculating 11, 66
Arizona 3, 11, 96, 100, 114
Army Corps of Engineers 115
Asia 7, 17, 19, 34, 40, 67–68, 90, 92, 96
Aswan Dam 64
Atacama Desert 6
Atlantic Ocean 10, 18, 31, 34, 50, 79, 86, 93
    ENSO in 39
Attila 67
Australia 34, 41, 71, 82, 119
Australian Desert 6, 17
axis of rotation 6
    and seasons 6, 7
    tilt of 6, 7
Aztec Empire 99–100

B

bacteria 20, 109, 110, 111
Baltimore 76
Bangladesh 93
barley 96, 98
Basel 109
beans 96, 100
Benguela Current 34
biological oxygen demand 111
birch tree 51
Bitis peringueyi 20
blizzards 21
black 77
blocking 47–51, 49, *49*, 50

anticyclones (highs) 50
 in lee of mountains 50
cyclones (lows) 50
patterns in 51
"blood rain" 72, 74
Boerhaavia repens 16–17
boiling temperature 25, 27
Boise City 77
Bombay 65, 89
 rainfall in 87–88
 temperature in 88
Bonn 109
boojum tree 17
borehole 62, 64, 102
Brazil 42
 Current 34
Britain 2, 47, 50, 72, 74 *see also* England, Scotland
 definition of drought in 64
 significance of drought in 65
Bronicki, Lucien 115
Bureau of Dry Land Agriculture 95
Bureau of Reclamation 114
Burkina Faso 1, 83, 85
Burma 92
burrowing 19

C

cacti 17, 18, 20, 53
calcium hydroxide 110
California 41, 65, 73, 79, 98, 114, 116
 Current 34
camel 19, 70
Camelford 111
Canada 34, 35, 77
capillarity 56–59, *58*, 103
capillary fringe 56, 59
capillary matting 58–59
carbohydrates 14
 oxidation of 18
carbon, activated 110

carbonates 61
carbon dioxide 17, 18, 54, 109, 110, 123, 124
carpet viper 20
car wash *106*
cash crops 84–85
Caspian Sea 67
cattle 2, 70, 81–82, 125
CCN *see* cloud condensation nuclei
Central American Desert 6
Cerastes cerastes 19–20
CFCs 123
Chad 1, 83, 85, 86
 Lake 69
Chang Jiang River 119
charcoal 110
Chepil, W.S. 76
Cherbourg 35
Chile 10, 37
China 41, 67, 73, 90, 93, 117, 119
chinampas 99–100, 104
chlorine 110, 111
chlorofluorocarbons *see* CFCs
chlorophyll 17
cholera 71, 109
climate classification 66
 Thornthwaite 66
climatic optimum 68
climatic warming 79, 121–125
cloud 29–30
 base 30
 condensation nuclei 28
 cover 10, 29
 droplets 5
 formation 5, 10, *28*, 29, 30, 123
coachwhip 17
coagulation 110, 111
coffee 82
Cologne 109
Colorado 3, 77, 80
condensation 5, 18, 19, 29, 30

latent heat of 26, 28, 29, 123
 level 28, 28, 30
Congo, Democratic Republic of 3, 4
continental climate 7
contingent (accidental) drought 65, 74
convection 5, 7, 8, 28, 28, 90
 cell 9
convergent evolution 20
copper sulfate 110
Coriolis, Gustave de 32
Coriolis effect 31, 32–33, *32, 33*, 44, 48, 91
 magnitude of 33
cork oak 54
corn 96, 100
 yields 42
Cornwall 111
Côte d'Ivoire 82, 85, 93
cotton 54, *70*, 84, 85, 100
cotyledons 18
covalent bond 26
creep erosion 75
creosote bush 18, 20
Crete 67
Crotalus cerastes 19–20
cyanobacteria 108
cyclone, blocking 50
cyclonic flow 49

D

dams 101, 116
Darwin 41
dehydration 15–16, 105, 112
Delhi 90
dengue fever 71
denkli 101
Department of the Interior, U.S. 114
depression 47, 50
desalination 112–116
 cost of 114
desertification *40*

devastating drought 65
dew 18, 99
    dewpoint temperature 5,
        27, 28
Diourbel 85
Dipodomys 20
Dodge City 78
doldrums 9–10
Domenigoni Valley Dam 116
Dordogne 69
drizzle 29, 30
drought, classification of
    64–66
dry adiabatic lapse rate 28,
    29
Dusseldorf 109
dust 14, 28, 72–73, 109
    clouds 76, 77, 80
    particles, size of 72
    storm 72–73, 75, 75, 77,
        79, 80
Dust Bowl 2, 47, 73, 76–82,
    78, *80*
    and drought cycle 80, 82
    and drought prediction
        82
dysentery 109

E

earth dam 117–118, *118*
East Australia Current 34
Easter Island 37, 38
Echis carinatus 20
ecliptic, plane of 4, *4*, 6
Edmonton 3–4
effective precipitation 10
Egypt 64, 100, 101
    ancient 67, 102
Ein Bokek 115
Ekman, V.W. 31
Ekman effect 31
electricity generation 115,
    117
electrodialysis 113, 114

El Niño 38–39, 82 *see also*
    ENSO
        Index 41–42, *41*
energy, solar 4, 20, 92
England 47, 68, 69, 111
    droughts in 68, 72,
        124–125
    temperature records for
        51
    wine production in 68
Engraulis ringens 37
Enlarged Homestead Act,
    1909 96
ENSO 39, 40, 41, 42, 47, 51,
    71, 82
    prediction 42
enzymes 15
ephemerals 17
equator, climatic 7, 23, 90
equatorial climate 4, 5, 6, 7
equinoxes 7
Eremitalpa granti 19
Eritrea 71
Eschscholzia minutiflora 17
Ethiopia 1, 63, 70–71, 82, 83,
    93
Euphorbiaceae 17, 18, 20
Euphrates 66, 101
Europe 2, 34, 40, 47, 50, 51,
    54, 67, 68, 69, 73, 86, 95,
    108
evaporation 4, 5, 10, 27, 28,
    29, 30, 37, 51–52, 53, 54,
    55, 56, 58, 65, 103, 104,
    113, 123, 124
    latent heat of 26, 37, 123
    rate of 10, 15, 17, 53, 59,
        72, 119
    reducing 18, 96, 98
    in reservoirs 119
evapotranspiration 51, 59
    potential 66
evergreen plants 53

F

Fairbanks 3
famine 55, 68, 70, 71, 93
farming 94
    chinampas 99–100
    dry 96–99
    fallow 95–96, 98
    Hohokam 100, 103
    Hopi 96
    Nabatean 102
fault 14, 60
feces, water content of 105,
    106
fennec 20
Fennecus zerda 20
Ferrel, William 9
ferric chloride 110
ferric sulfate 110
Fertile Crescent 100–101
Finland 47
fire 2
    forest 3
flocculation *see* coagulation
floods 10, 38, 41, 55, 70, 93
    preventing 116, 118, 119
Florida 114
    Current 31
fluorine 26
food production, global 82
fog 30, 34
foggaras 101
Fouquieria splendens 17
France 35, 47, 68–69, 109
freeboard 117
freezing 26, 34, 113, 114
    latent heat of 26, 114
    temperature 25, 29, 30
front 28, *28*, 47 *see* also in-
    tertropical front and polar
    front

G

Gabon 89
gecko 19

Germany 109
glaciers 27, 112
global warming 41, 42
Grant's desert mole 19
grasses, prairie 77–78, 79, 96
gravel 13, 14, 59, 98
Great Depression 79
Great Lakes 107
Great Plains 50, 51, 77, 80, 82, 95
Greece 67
greenhouse effect 122–125
Greenland 22, 24, 34
   precipitation 22
gross national product 83
groundwater 13–14, 56, 57, 59, 60, 62–63, 71, 85, 101, 102, 104, 107
   abstraction 64
   contamination 103, 109
   flow 59, 60, 61, 62, 71
guano 37
Guinea Bissau 84
Gulf Stream 31, 34
gyres 31

H

Hadley cells 9, 11, 23, 31, 43, 46, 86
Hadley, George 9
Halley, Edmund 9
Harappa 67
Hawaii 41
heat capacity 11–12
Himalayas 90, 91
Hohokam people 100, 103
holly 53
Homestead Act, 1862 78, 94, 96
Hoover Dam 116
Hopi farming 96
horned viper 19–20
Humboldt Current *see* Peru Current
Hunni 67

Hwang Ho 73
hydrochloric acid 25
hydroelectric plants 117
hydrogen 25, 26
   bond 26, 27, 53, 56, 57, 73, 113

I

ice 21, 24, 27, 112, 113
   age 73, 122
   bergs 21, 113
   crystals 29, 30
   sheet 21, 22, 73, 123
      thickness of 21, 22
Iceland 68
Idaho 96
Idria columnaris 17
Ilex 53
impermeable rock *13*, 14
India 6, 36, 41, 65, 86, *88*, 90, 91, 93, *95*, 101, 116
   definition of drought in 64
Indian Ocean 10, 31, 37
Indonesia 37, 38, 40, 71
Indus Valley 67
In Salah 11
International Monetary Fund 71
intertropical convergence 70, 87, 90, 91, 92, 93
intertropical front 46
invisible drought 65–66
Iowa 79, *81*
Iquique 10
Iraq 66, 101
irrigation 54, 65, *70*, 94, *95*, 96, *97*, 100–104, 118, 121
   dangers of 103
   extent of 104
isobars 44, 45
Israel 41, *41*, 42, 97, *97*, 101–102, 114, 115
   rainfall in 96
Italy 108, 116
Ivory Coast *see* Côte d'Ivorie

J

Jaculus 20
Jakarta 71
Japan 34, 67, 92
jerboas 20
jet stream 46, 47, 90 *see also* polar front jet stream and subtropical front jet stream

K

Kalahari Desert 19
kangaroo rats 18, 20
Kansas 2, 77, 78, 79, 80, 95
Kariba Dam 117
Karlsruhe 109
Kenya 82
Key West 114
Kibbutz en Gedi 97
Kisangani 3, 4
kit fox 20
Koblenz 109
Kodiak Island 35
Korea 67
Kuroshio Current 34, 40
Kuwait 114

L

Labrador Current 34
lakes, Antarctic 21
Lancang River 117
La Niña 40
Larrea divaricata 18
latent heat 26–27, 28, 29, 37 *see also* condensation, evaporation, melting, and sublimation
leaves 51, 52, 53, 54
lenticels 51
Lhasa 90
Libreville 89
lichens 20, 24
light intensity 14–15, 52–53
Lima 37, *40*

Little Ice Age 68, 69, 70, 122, 125
lizards 19
loess 73
London 69, 125
    Great Fire of 69
Los Angeles 116
Ludwigshafen 109

M

McCoy, Isaac 79–80
Mainz 109
Mali 1, 3, 4, 69–70, 83, 85
Mandingo Empire 69
Mannheim 109
Manwan Dam 117
Mather, J.R. 66
Mauritania 1, 83, 85
Mead, Lake 116
Mekong River 117
melons 96
melting, latent heat of 26
Mennonites 95
meridional flow 47, 49
methane 25, 123
Mexico 100
    City 99
Miami 93
Midi 69
midlatitudes 7, 43, 90, 92
migration 85
millet 96
Mississippi River 73
Missouri *1*, 3
    River 73
Mohenjo-Daro 67
moisture index 66
monsoon 1, 2, 36, 37, 41, 64, 65, 85, 87–94
    African 93
    American 93
    Asian 92, 93, 123
    Indian 89–92
    reliability of 93-94
    summer 90, 91, 92, 93

    winter *88*, 90, 92, 93
Montana 77
Morocco 70, *70*, 71
mosses 20, 24
Mozambique 84, 93
mudslide 38, 118
mulch 98
multistage flash evaporation 114

N

Nabateans 101–102
NADW *see* North Atlantic Deep Water
Nagasaki 92
Namib Desert 18, 19
Namibia *16, 75*
Nebraska 79, 80
Negev Desert 101–102
Netherlands 109
Nevada 116
New China Dam 119
Newfoundland 34
New Mexico 3, 77
New York 76
    water use in 120–121
Niger 1, 83, 85
    rainfall in 85
    river 70
Nigeria 82, 93
Nile River 64, 67, 116
nitrates 108
nitrogen 26
    oxides 109
nitrous oxide 123
nomads 1, 67, 84, 96
North American deserts 17, 18, 20
North Atlantic Deep Water 34–35
North Atlantic Drift 34, 35
North Equatorial Current 31, 34
North Pole 23
North Sea 109

Norway 34, 68
Norwegian Current 34, 35

O

Oahe Dam 116
oases 13–14, *13*, 60, 101
ocean 3, 4, 59, 123, 124
    currents 31–35, 36, 42
ocotillo 17
Ogaden 71
Ohio 77
oil prices 83
Oimyakon 23
Oklahoma 2, 77, 80, 82
Opuwo 75
orbit of Earth 7
Oregon 96
orographic lifting 28
osmosis *15*, 105, 112
    reverse 113, 114
overgrazing 85, 87
oxygen 17, 18, 25, 26, 54, 110
    dissolved 111–112
Oyashio Current 34
ozone 110, 123
    layer 82

P

Pacific anchovy 37
Pacific Ocean 10, 31, 34, 37, 38, 39, 40, 42, 79
paecottah 101
Palestine 67
Palmatogecko rangei 19
Palouse region 96
Paraguay 116
Paraná River 116
paratyphoid fever 109
partially permeable membrane *15*, 113
pasture 1, 84, 85, 87
pastoralists 84–85, 87
peanuts 82

peas 51, 96
Pennsylvania 11, 12, *106*
Pepys, Samuel 69
Perigueux 69
permanent drought 65, 69
permeable rock 13, 14
Peru 37, *40*
    Current 34, 37, 38
    fisheries 37, 38, 39, *39*,
        40, 41, 82
    rainfall in 38
Philadelphia 11, 12, *106*
Phoenix 11
    water use in 121
phosphates 108
photosynthesis 14–15, 17,
    52, 53, 54
    at high temperature 18
    at low temperature 24
phytoplankton 37
pine trees 42
plague 69
planetary vorticity 48–49, 50
plants 2, 94
    crop 94, 103
    desert 16–18, 53, 94
plastic sheeting 98–99
Podor 85
Point MacKenzie 3
polar air 47
polar deserts 6, 20–24
polar front *8*, 9, 21, 46, 47,
    48, 50
    jet stream 46, 47, 49, 50
    position of 46
polar high 43, 92
polar molecule 26, 56, 57
poles, climatic 23
poliomyelitis 109
pomegranates 96–97
Poolewe 35
potassium permanganate 110
potential evapotranspiration
    66
pressure gradient 45
    force 44

proteins 15

Q

Quercus cerris 54
Quercus subur 54

R

radioactive decay 21
railroads 94, 95
rainfall 2, 5, 37, 38, 54, 55,
    58, 59, 71, 74, 116, 123, 124
    and drought 65–66, 72
    desert 10, 11, 13
    distribution 3, 11, 55, 74
    during an ENSO 40, 41
    and farming 95–99
    in Great Plains 77, 78,
        79, 80
    in the Sahel 84, 85
    tropical 89
rain forest 89
rain shadow 7, 13
rainwater 109
Red River 115
Red Sea 93
reforestation *40*
relative humidity 5, 28, 29,
    30, 52, 53
relative vorticity 48, 49
reptiles 19
Republican River 79–80
reservoirs 2, 65, 72, 118–119,
    120
    and recreation 120
respiration 14, 17, 24, 103
    releasing water 18, 105
Rharb Valley 70
Rhine 73, 109
rice 82, 88
riprap 117
rivers 10, 55, 56, 59, 65, 71,
    72, 109, 117, 119
Rocky Mountains 7, 50, 79
Rogun Dam 116

Roman Empire 67, 107–108,
    116
Rome 108
roots 51, 53, 54, 96, 103, 104
    and erosion 74
Rossby, Carl-Gustav 40, 48
Rossby waves 40, 48, 49, 49
Royal Botanic Gardens 50
Russia 40, 41, 50, 82, 83, 117

S

Sahara Desert 1, 6, 11, 13,
    20, 40, 50, 69, 70, 83, 87
    cloud cover in 10
    dust from 72
    irrigation in 101
Sahel 1–2, 40, 47, 50, 70,
    82–87, 84
St. Louis 3–4
salinization 103
    remedying 103–104
salt 28, 34, 103, 112
    -gradient solar pond 115
    solution 34, 35, 112
saltation 75
Salt River 100
San Antonio 2, 80
sand 13, 14, 20
    boas 19
    dunes 16
    grains 73, 75, 76 *see*
        also soil particles
    heat capacity of 12
    storms 73, 75
San Diego 65, 116
San Joaquin Valley 73
Santa Ana River 116
Sargon 66
saturated adiabatic lapse rate
    28
saturation 5, 27, 29, 30, 52
    of soil 56, 58, 59, 60
    vapor pressure 52
Saudi Arabia 93, 114
Scandinavia 50

scattering of light 72
scorpions 19
Scotland 35
Scott, Captain Robert 20
seasonal drought 65
seasons 6, 7
    rainy 65, 70, 87, 93 *see also* monsoon
    tropical 88–89
sea-surface temperature 37, 38, 40, 42, 124
Secota 63
sedimentation 119
seeds 16
seepage line 118, 118
semipermeable membrane *see* partially permeable membrane
Senegal 1, 84, 85
    rainfall in 85
Seven Oaks Dam 116
sewage 108, 111, 112
shaduf 101
shelter belts 82
Shewa 70
Siberia 23
Sicily 102
sidewinder rattlesnake 19–20
Silk Road 67
skinks 19
Skye, Isle of 2
smallpox 68
smoke 3
snakes 19
snow 20, 21, 27, 55, 58, 59, 80, 123
    fall, measuring 21–22
    fields 27
    flakes 28
sodium thiosulfate 110
soil 55
    cultivation 95
    desert 17
    erodibility 76
    erosion 55, 73–79, 87, 96
    extent of 76, 79, 80

particles 54, 55–57, 58, 59, 73, 74–75, 76, 109, 119
    clay 55–56
sand 55–56
silt 55–56, 109, 119
Soil Conservation Service 79
solarization 15
solar radiation cycle 82
solar spectrum 122
Somalia 71
soot 109
sorghum 82, 96
Sousevlei 16
South Dakota 116
South Equatorial Current 31, 34, 37, 38
Southern Oscillation 37, 38, 39, 51
    Index 41–42
South Pole 23
soybeans 81
Spanish oak 54
Spitzbergen 79
spring 60, *61*, 61, 104, 106
    temperature of water from 61
sprinkler 102
spurges 17, 18, 20
squashes 96, 100
Sri Lanka 116
stomata 17, 18, 51, 53, 54
storm 21, 47
    cloud 29, 30
    track 47
Strasbourg 109
stratosphere 82, 86
sublimation 27, 29, 30
    latent heat of 26
subtropical air 47
subtropical anticyclone 8, 43, 50, 90, 92
subtropical front jet stream 46, 90
subtropics 4, 23, 37, 92, 123
    deserts in 6, 7

succulents 17
Sudan 1, 83, 96
sulfate 28
sulfur dioxide 109, 123
sunspots 82
supersaturation 28, 29
surface tension 57, 58
sweating 15, 19, 105, 106
Sweden 47
Switzerland 109
Syracuse 102
Syria 66, 101

T

Tahiti 41
Tajikistan 116
taproot 18
Taranto 108
Tell Leilan 66–67
temperate climate 4, 53, 123
Tenochtitlán-Tlatelolco *see* Mexico City
terracing 97–98, *98*, 99, 102
Texas 2, 73, 77, 80, 81, 115
Texcoco, Lake 99
Thailand 92
Thames River 69, 125
Thar Desert 6
thorns 18
Thornthwaite, C.W. 66
Three Gorges 119
Thule 22
Tiber River 108
Tibet 90
Tibetan Plateau 90, 91, 92, 93
Tigray 70, 71
Tigris River 66, 101, 116
Timbuktu 3, 4, 69–70
Topex-Poseidon satellite 42
trade winds 8–9, 10, 31, 36, 37, 38, 40, 86, 87, 90, 91, 93
transpiration 51, 52, 53, 54, 55, 65, 95
trees 53
    broadleaved 53

coniferous 53
    deciduous 53
tropical air 50
tropical cyclones 124
Tropic of Cancer 6, 91
Tropic of Capricorn 6, 91
tropics *4*, 6, 37, 40, 92, 123
tropopause 6, 36, 46
troposphere 82
Tsin Dynasty 67
Tucson, water use in 121
turgidity 53
Turkey oak 54
typhoid fever 109

U

ultraviolet radiation 82
United Nations Environment
    Program 85
United States 2, 7, 41, 47, 68,
    83, 86, 93, 96
    cost of water 114
    dams in 116
    definition of drought in
        64
    desalination in 114
    expansion of farming in
        94–95
    industrial water use in
        107, 121
    water consumption in
        121
upwelling 37, 38
urine 19, 105
Uttar Pradesh *88*, 95

V

vacuum freezing 114–115
Vakhsh River 116
Vancouver 35
vapor pressure 52–53
    and temperature 52
Verkhoyansk 23
    climate 23

veterinary care 84
Vietnam 92
viruses 109, 111
Volga River 117
Volgograd Dam 116–117
volunteer plants 95
vorticity 31, 48
Vostok, Lake 21
Vostok station 21
Vulpes velox 20

W

Wadi Halfa 10
Walker, Sir Gilbert 36
Walker circulation 36
Washington, D.C. 55, 76
Washington State 96
water 3, 5, 24
    acidity 109, 110
    biological need for
        14–19, 24, 51–55, 94,
        104–106
    for chemical transport
        53, 94
    conserving 97–98,
        120–121
    cycle 3, 55, 112
    density 34
        and temperature 34
    domestic use 107, 109,
        120
    drainage 56, 60, 104
    drinking 104–105, 107,
        109
        amount needed
            105–106
    droplets 28, 29, 30, 55
        supercooled 29–30
    hardness 61, 110
    heat capacity of 11–12
    industrial use 107, 109
    in soil 50, 51, 53, 54,
        55–57, 65
    management 100

molecule 25–27, 25, 28,
    29, 52, 53, 56, 73, 103,
    113
    residence time, in
        ocean 59
    phases of 24–25
    pollution 108, 110–111
    purification 106, 108,
        109–112
    recycling 107, 109, 121
    restrictions on use 2
    salt contamination of 103
    soft 61
    storage 116–119
    stress 54
    supply 106–107, 109
    table 56, 57, 59, 60, 62,
        63, 64, 65, 85, 102, 103,
        104
    vapor 5, 6, 17, 24–25, 27,
        28, 29, 30, 52, 55, 123,
        124
        supercooled 29
waterlogging 60, 103, 104
weather systems, midlatitude
    7
weeds 95, 98, 99
Weizmann Institute of Sci-
    ence 42
well *61*, 61–62, *63*, 101, 103,
    106, 109
    artesian (overflowing)
        61, 62, 64
    size of 62, 71
    temperature of water
        from 61, 62
Welo 70
welwitschia 18
Welwitschia mirabilis 18
West Wind Drift 34
wheat 54, 70, 78, 80–81, 82,
    83, 96
    area growing 78
White House 76
wildlife 2, 119
    desert 14, 16–20, 53

polar 24
wilting 51, 53
wind 20, 21, 27, 34, 124 *see also* trade winds
  breaks 82, 96
  and dust 73
  erodibility equation 76
  and friction 44, 74
  geostrophic 44
  lifting power of 76
  patterns, global *43*, 43–44
  prevailing 44, 47, 86, 90, 92

and soil erosion 73, 74, 74, 75, 76, 80
  thermal 46
wine harvest 68
Woodruff, N. P. 76

X

xerophytes 53
Xochimilco, Lake 99, 100

Y

Yakir, Dan 42

Yangtze River *see* Chang Jiang River
Yacyretá-Apipe Dam 116
Yellow River *see* Hwang Ho
Yuma Desalting Plant 114

Z

Zambesi River 117
Zambia 117
Zimbabwe 42, 117
zonal flow 47, 48, 49